ALL IRELAND

ALL
IRELAND

EDITED BY JONATHAN MOORE

CHARTWELL
BOOKS, INC.

Published by Chartwell Books
A Division of Book Sales, Inc.
110 Enterprise Avenue
Secaucus, New Jersey 07094

ISBN 1-55521-072-4
Reprinted 1989
This book was designed and produced by
QUINTET PUBLISHING LIMITED
6 Blundell Street
London N7 9BH

ART DIRECTOR: Peter Bridgewater
DESIGNER: Linda Henley
EDITORS: Shaun Barrington, Robert Stewart
Photography by Trevor Wood, assisted by Jonathan Higgins

Typeset in Great Britain by
Central Southern Typesetters, Eastbourne
Manufactured in Hong Kong by
Regent Publishing Services Limited
Printed in Hong Kong by South Sea Int'l Press Ltd

CONTENTS

RIGHT *From Kerry to Donegal, along the Atlantic seaboard, Ireland's most dramatic scenery is concentrated. The harsh, unyielding rocky landscape, with only the thinnest covering of vegetation, contrasts with the ever shifting liquid sky.*

CENTRE *Thatched cottages, like this one in Galway, are more commonly found in the far west of Ireland, far from urban encroachment.*

FAR RIGHT *The landscape of Connemara is scarred by the efforts of generations of Irishmen and women to wrest peat from the soil.*

• INTRODUCTION •

There is a richness and diversity about the Irish experience which cautions any writer against bland simplifications and stereotypes. How can one make sweeping generalizations about a people who throughout most of their history have been poor and lived on the land and yet have produced some of the greatest writers the world has ever known.

That paradox is at the heart of Irish history. Ireland has been economically poor for most of its history, 'a pocket of un-development in an advanced region,' as Oliver MacDonagh has observed, and yet for all its poverty, hardship and suffering, it has produced a culture of abiding strength.

For many, the vast, beautiful scenery of Connaught in the west is the real Ireland. It is there that the inner qualities of the Irish are to be found, as founder of the Gaelic League, Douglas Hyde, remarked in 1926. 'Remember that the best of our people were driven by Cromwell to hell or Connacht ... They are men and women of the toughest fibre. They have been for generations fighting with the sea, fighting with the weather, fighting with the mountains. They are, indeed, the survival of

the fittest. Give them but half a chance and they are the seeds of a great race ... It will save the historical Irish nation for it will preserve for all time the fountain-source from which further generations can draw for ever.'

Such a vision of the real Ireland will appeal to all who have travelled to the west. The beauty of Connemara, the stark, rugged nature of its landscape and the dignity, warmth and honesty of the people invite us to see this as the real Ireland. In reality, it is but one piece in a much larger jigsaw. The beauty of rural Ireland is that it coexists, cheek by jowl, with the many other aspects of Ireland, each of which has an equal, if differing appeal.

The cultural strength of the Irish is most famed in literature. How is it that a country so small, so rural and so poor has produced geniuses such as Yeats, Shaw, Wilde, Kavanagh, Synge, Joyce and Heaney? The English are forever trying to adopt these writers as their own. But, despite their different styles, views, backgrounds and religion, these writers have something clearly and unmistakably Irish about them.

The rural and literary traditions in Irish life are two of the many areas that are explored in this book, which is intended to

introduce people to the many different facets of being Irish. Underlying every section is one common theme, namely, that the greatest natural resource that the Irish nation possesses is its people. Not even the greatest Irish patriot could boast about Ireland's mineral resources; neither could it be said that the climate is always to one's liking (although the rain is said to be softer than in any other part of the globe). But the people, not an homogenous population, retain, for all their diversity, something inextricably Irish.

The question of what constitutes being a member of a 'race' or 'nation' is of great pertinence in the Irish case. Since the 19th century there has been a constant flow of Irish men and women abroad; only the diaspora of the Jews can rival it. Driven out of their country by hunger and poverty, the Irish have become a genuinely international race. At the time of the birth of the Irish Free State in 1921, more than 40 per cent of Irish-born men and women were living abroad. The effect of this has been that the Irish have been able to make a contribution to life often thousands of miles from the Emerald Isle. This book is dedicated to those millons of people who see themselves as Irish, but who may have never even travelled to the old country. We hope that the material in the book will give you some flavour of what constitutes the Irish experience.

Irish
Rural
Life

The cliffs of Portrush on the northern coast;
Portrush is one of Ulster's most popular
tourist areas.

ABOVE AND NEAR RIGHT *Flower gardens are an unusual sight in the west of Ireland, where the weather is hostile to fragility and the land has always been viewed as a provider of sustenance. Potted flowers are a common sight on the sills of the neat cottages; the windowsill was often the only corner of a cottage secure against the foraging of hens and other farmyard animals*

TOP AND BOTTOM, FAR RIGHT *Reminders of a bygone way of life: the horse trough (TOP), and the village pump (BOTTOM), in County Wexford, a relic now, but still deemed worthy of a regular coat of new paint. In spite of all the rain, drinking water was often a problem for Irish families. Springs were first pumped into the farmyards to provide a regular supply towards the end of the 19th century; when village pumps replaced the open wells, they quickly became a local meeting place.*

Since 1847, when the Famine so cruelly depopulated the countryside, the rural landscape of Ireland has been changing. Disappearing slowly but surely have been the traditional, three-roomed cabins with their thatched roofs, settle beds and open turf fires – a hollow scooped out each side for cat and dog. In their place has grown up a new generation of bungalows, individual in the extreme, whose pantile roofs, aluminium window frames, pillared gateways and fluted-glass front doors cause not a little offence to the city-bound purists who would preserve the idea, if not the reality, of the rare oul' times. To the stranger the sight of the little thatched homesteads being superseded by the smart new bungalows might seem a sad one but, contrary to what the sociologists might have us think, there is no great conflict between the two, for transition is slow in Ireland and no one is more than a generation or two away from the days when milk came straight from the cow and water from a well. The smell of a cowshed, the steam rising from a horse's flank, the curl of turfsmoke from a small, white-washed chimney – these images, celebrated in many an exile's song lie close to the surface of the Irish consciousness, keeping the nation in touch with a rural reality lost to less fortunate, industrialized countries.

Nowadays, milk comes in green, white and orange packs, courtesy of An Born Bainne, the national dairy board. Out along the country roads, the hedges bejewelled in summer with purple, pink and red fuschia, can be seen the wooden platforms where the farmers leave their churns to be picked up by a lorry and taken to the local creamery. There, the cream is taken off and the milk churned into butter and cheese, leaving behind the buttermilk – that magic ingredient which makes soda bread, spread with yellow, Kerrygold butter, a meal in itself. Milk from the national herd turns up in odd places these days, in cream liqueurs and even in Irish cheddar – which is exported to England!

For children born and bred in Dublin – Jackeens as they are called – the countryside takes a bit of getting used to. With an arrogance typical of your average Dubliner, anywhere outside the city is referred to simply as 'the country', regardless of whether it is Kerry, Cork or the west. A child packed off to boarding school in Athlone, a major midland town set in the very heartland of rural Ireland, would set off in a single-decker bus from the Liffey quays, and would soon be bouncing and rattling along the bumpy roads, slowing down to go through

the towns of Kinnegad, Tyrell's Pass, Kilbeggan, Horseleap and Moate, their streets wide and open to accommodate the weekly cattle market. Somewhere along the route the road would start to switch back, sending shabby cardboard cases and brown paper parcels tumbling down from the luggage rack – for this was Ireland's subterranean powerhouse, the great Bog of Allen. Then the journey would continue down to the broad, flat floodplains of the Shannon, Ireland's longest river, and into Athlone, the birthplace of the tenor, John McCormack. (Here, in 1691, 20 Irishmen died in a spectacularly brave, but vain, attempt to cut off the advancing forces of William of Orange by dismantling, plank by plank, the wooden bridge across the Shannon.)

Things have greatly improved, of course, since those days of the rickety country bus. With its entry into the European Economic Community, Ireland has attracted a number of public service improvement grants and the road from Dublin to Athlone is now smooth and straight – almost – and runs right on through to Galway. Crossing over today's bridge of Athlone you pass into Connaught, that craggy and most enduring of the four provinces, the one to which Oliver Cromwell, in the 1640s, banished the Irish who got in his way. You know you are in Connaught by the low, stone walls that mark out the many small fields which turn the landscape into a patchwork of deep, rich browns and bright, shining greens.

'The curse of Cromwell on you' the people still say in exasperation, when everyday things go wrong – and in a farming community there are many things that can go wrong, not least of them the famous Irish weather. 'La brea bog' they say ('a fine, soft day') when the sun is shining and people are out with their forks, turning the hay to dry before making it up into neat haycocks. Country people talk about 'saving' the hay and 'winning' the turf, for rural life is a difficult and continual struggle fought on many fronts. In summer, round about the time of the Munster hurling finals, Tipperary people, if they have been victorious, may be heard to remark, 'It's a great day altogether, thanks be to God, for we have the hay saved and Cork bet' – a reference to the annual sporting battle between those two great counties.

The real battle in the Irish countryside, however, is fought with the elements. 'It's not us that does the farming,' a farmer will say, looking up anxiously at a sky looming with rain. 'It's the weather.' When the sun does shine, everyone works hell for leather. Whole families take to the fields – cousins home from England, the brother back from America, the uncle over

ABOVE *The Ring of Kerry in the south west: the coastline from Parknasilla to Glenbeigh is punctuated by enormous beaches.*

In the 19th century, Ireland was very thoroughly surveyed. The smallest unit of occupation was, and still is, a townland. There are about 60,000 townlands in Ireland, mostly about half an acre in size, each harbouring anything from two to six homesteads. Neighbouring townlands will help each other at harvest time and during the height of the season the man most in demand is the farmer with a tractor, mower and trailer. He will be out working for his neighbours every daylight hour, leaving only the night for him to get his own hay in. The spirit of cooperation comes easily to a people whose material resources are in relatively short supply and who still remember hard times. Ireland is dotted with cooperatives set up by the farmers themselves.

Where before the weekly mart was held in the street, with cattle, sheep, dogs and people all milling round together in wind, hail or rain, now the local cooperative will have built a large, covered auction ring with offices and toilets attached. By seven in the morning, on market days, the narrow roads leading to the town are filled with tractors and trailers toing and froing between mart and farm. Men congregate on street corners, leaning on their sticks, their dogs lying dutifully at their feet. Palms are spat upon and hands shaken on the completion of a deal. The traditional dinner – a large steaming plate of cabbage, spuds and steak – is served throughout the day alongside the offerings from the local fast-food joint, for the American influence is only a parish away and even the smallest of Irish towns has its Texas Burger Bar or Uncle Sam's Steak Counter.

The nub of the fair, however, is the bar, open all day, and packed with farmers and dealers, flat caps pulled down over lean faces eroded by the wind; men who joke about the huge rolls of notes they carry with them – 'Now which pocket is it at all that I keep the hundred pound notes in?' Small boys, the sons or grandsons of the pub, scurry about dragging in crates of Guinness and Smithwicks from the yard, for the shelves must be replenished as soon as they show any signs of drying up.

And it is not only the farmers who keep their notes in hundred pound rolls. Fishermen, too, have a way of counting their money like that, for while farmers reap the fruits of the land so fishermen reap the harvest of the ocean. No part of Ireland is more than 60 miles from the sea and along the west coast in particular, the farming and fishing traditions have always been linked. On many a country pub counter, you will find a saucer of some variety of seaweed, put there for you to chew on. In the old days, dulse, caragean moss and iodine-rich kelp were eaten with potatoes which were used, in very hard

from Australia. Everyone lends a hand for it would be a lean winter if the cattle had no food and the family no turf. Nowadays, the sale of turf briquettes, machine-cut and dried by Bord Na Mona, the national turf board, makes things easier, but a wet summer can still mean disaster, for no ordinary tractor can get up to the bog and what remains of the last year's turf must go to the hospitals and power stations, which have first call on this most vital of Ireland's resources. There are nearly three million acres of bogland in Ireland and her expertise in this field is now being exported to peat-producing countries such as Burundi and Senegal. Dublin airport, in fact, is a good example of the old giving to the new, for its boilerhouses are powered by turf.

ABOVE *The bleak and imposing bogland of Connemara; perhaps the most immediately identifiable image of Ireland.*

FAR LEFT *Kerry is the heartland of Irish dairy farming, in the south west of the island. Irish life from earliest times has revolved around the herding of cattle, and the drover is still as familiar a figure today as he was in the ancient Celtic sagas.*

LEFT *Many of the smallholders in the west rear calves until they are old enough to be sold at cattle fairs to graziers from the large farms of Meath.*

The popular image of Irish food is of a diet of bacon and cabbage, potatoes, strong tea and soda bread – and these ingredients do indeed feature in Irish cooking. But it is not the whole story by a long way. Ireland, for a small and not particularly rich country, has traditionally enjoyed a very varied diet. The ancient writings abound with references to meat of all kind. Beef, dairy produce, fatted calf – veal – and other meats were very common, as one might expect in a country where the whole wealth of society was expressed in terms of cattle. Pottage, or hash, made from finely chopped meat mixed with sprouts and flavoured with herbs was a particular feature. Mutton, poultry and eggs have always been available, as part of a small farm economy. In the seventeenth century the planting of large numbers of Scots in Ulster

introduced oaten bread and porage, while the English from the west country settling in Munster increased the amount of cereals grown and brought about a corresponding rise in bread production. These settlers also brought with them a taste for cider, planting orchards on their Irish estates.

The Gaelic tradition, on the other hand, with its dependence on herding cattle, required a more mobile life style and wild berries, cresses and fruit were used to supplement a meat diet. In a country so abundant with forests, lakes and rivers, fishing and hunting provided both a recreation and an important source of food.

It was not until the massive population growth of the late eighteenth and early nineteenth century that the poorer classes were forced to a greater dependence on the potato, but this dependence was only among the very poor. A widely varied diet of meats, dairy produce and vegetables was still consumed by all other classes. As the population fell after the great Famine of the 1840s, mainly through the emigration of labourers and the poorer farmers, the statistics for dairy and meat production per head of the population began to rise so that today it is one of the highest anywhere. Dublin Bay prawns are of course a delicacy enjoyed all over the world.

ABOVE *Traditional Irish soda bread, made with buttermilk and deeply scored with a cross before baking.*

FAR LEFT *The gradual increase in the amount of cereal grown in Ireland during the 18th century resulted in the replacement of rushes by straw for animal bedding and thatch.*

LEFT *Hard times: seaweed not used for fertilizer, but for food, in the 1880s.*

times, to pay the rent. Up to recent times, along the west coast, where top soil is in short supply, plants were actually grown in beds of seaweed.

In times gone by, too, the sea presented a threat to people living along the Atlantic coast, especially the people of Tir Conaill, perhaps better known as Donegal – the 'Fort of the Foreigner'. The foreigner was the land-hungry Viking, who came surging in on the crest of the Atlantic wave to take what he could from the fearful people of Donegal. Only on stormy nights could they rest easy in their beds.

Bitter the wind tonight,
Combing the sea's hair white:
from the North, no need to fear
the proud sea-coursing warrior.

That was all long ago and today Ireland's fishermen – and a few women skippers too – can earn a sizable income though, crafty people that they are, they are the last to admit it.

If you drive along the coastal road from Donegal Town to Killybegs, Ireland's premier fishing port, and take a walk around the harbour there, you will see a prosperity never dreamed of a hundred years ago. Huge, deep-sea trawlers line up with small inshore boats to roam the seas from Donegal Bay to Norway, returning with their catch of cod, whiting, herring and mackerel, which are processed in Killybegs or driven down in great refrigerated trucks to the Dublin fishmarkets.

The county of Donegal is a legend in itself. Cut off from the rest of Ireland by rivers and mountains, it has retained an aspect of the Irish character which its critics describe as anarchic and its admirers call independent. One of the three Ulster counties located in the republic, it encapsulates both the traditions and the changing spirit of rural Ireland. Against a mountainous backdrop of purple and green, lit by the brilliance of an Atlantic sunset, or lashed by violent winds and thunderous rain, small thatched houses sit snug into the comforting protection of a hillside, their chimneys smoking peacefully. Nearby stand the new bungalows with their fitted kitchens, carports and flowerless gardens of green grass. In the country a garden usually means a patch near the homestead where staple vegetables such as cabbages, potatoes and scallions are cultivated by the woman of the house. It is only recently that the frivolity of growing something as unproductive as flowers has seeped into this stoney county.

LEFT *The bicycle is still a common means of transport into town (here Westport, County Mayo) for those living on isolated farms who wish to pick up supplies.*

BELOW *The curragh is a light boat made of canvas and wood still used by islanders off the west coast for journeys to and from the mainland. Despite their apparent fragility, they were often used to transport cattle, which were tied up and placed in the bottom of the boat.*

ABOVE *Braving the freezing waters of the Atlantic at the Ring of Kerry.*

RIGHT *Road signs in Kilkenny: religion, art, leisure, the Gaelic language, all conveniently and symbolically grouped.*

Each year two-and-a-half million visitors come to Ireland and, soulless though some of the new bungalows may seem from the outside, if they have a B&B sign swinging at the door, you may be sure that inside the same, world-famous hospitality is still to be found. In the wilder, emptier parts of Ireland, most people will give you a wave of the hand whether they know you or not.

And out of the blending of purples, reds, greens and blues on the distant mountains come the county's other asset – its tweeds. Walking through a small town like Ardara, with its shop signs in the Irish language (for this is the Donegal Gaelthacht), you may hear the steady, rhythmic knock of wood against wood: the village weaver is at work in his tall weaving shed. Although not as numerous as they once were, weavers are still to be found in and around these parts and Donegal tweed is renowned both for its colour and its warmth. Recently there has been a revival in the skills of weaving and spinning. Women have been the leaders in this revival, either operating from their own kitchens or banding together in a rural coop.

Further along from Ardara, through the great Gilgesh Pass – this whole section of the Slieve League Peninsula is breathtaking in its isolated beauty – lies Kilcar, another tiny Gaelthacht town, where an attempt has been made to revitalise the economy by investing in traditional crafts. The tweed factory supplies exclusive weaves to the big fashion houses both in Ireland and abroad, and it also sells cloth direct from the loom to anyone sensible enough to call by. Just up the street from the factory is Columba Doherty, the local tailor. Sitting crosslegged on his broad workbench, surrounded by threads, buttons, pins and buckles, he is as happy making a set of jackets for the local Garda, whose uniform has recently been updated, as he is sewing a tweed coat for a visiting tourist. Named after Saint Columba, Donegal's great scholar, he is sadly the last of a line of people who traditionally held a position of considerable importance in the rural community.

One of the images of the Irish in exile is that of fighting, drinking, noisy countrymen – or rough, rug-headed kerns, as Shakespeare put it. Not too complimentary perhaps but, like all clichés, it contains an element of truth, for the majority of immigrants came from the great, west-coast counties of Ireland – Cork, Kerry, Donegal, Galway and Mayo – and they were familiar with the hardships of life, with trying to wrest a living from a windswept, unyielding land. As a result, the people of these counties have a vigour and a drive not often found among their city cousins. That vigour pervades every area of their lives

LEFT *This image of a farmhouse in the far west of Galway near Clifden, on the fringes of Europe, is strongly reminiscent of Thomas Girtin's famous watercolour. The White House, Chelsea; the building shines against the sombre greens in the clear Irish light, the kind of landscape which attracts many watercolourists to Ireland.*

ABOVE *The wild gorse of County Cork in the south blossoms in the early autumn.*

18

ABOVE Derelict cottages like this in the Ring of Kerry can be found all over Ireland. They are a witness to the generations that have fled the land, lonesome reminders to those that remain of relatives in England, Australia and North America.

RIGHT AND FAR RIGHT Looking toward Lough Swilly, near Letterkenny, in County Donegal. The city of Derry is not so far to the east, across the Lough, across the River Foyle and across the border, in a different county, and a different country. The Derryveagh, Glendowan and Blue Stack Mountains of Donegal are populated by sheep which sustain the tweed industry. A great deal of the land is ill-suited to any other agricultural application.

and they are as energetic in work and play as they are boisterous in their language.

The Irish immigrants took this vigour with them when they left for England, Australia, New Zealand, Canada and the United States. The men went to work on the railways, the sewers, the canals, or navigation systems (from where we get the Irish 'navvy'), and, more recently, the motorways; the women took jobs in the sweatshops, the hospitals, the kitchens and the bars. They took with them a will and a determination to survive which brought many of them to positions of power seldom enjoyed by those at the bottom of the pile. Next time you use some Tabasco sauce, have a look at the name on the label – McIlhenny, it says. In the 1860s, George Adair, a vindictive and much hated landlord, evicted more than 140 people from his Glenveagh estate in north Donegal. Most of those evicted managed to get away to Australia, but some went to America. Adair put all his money and energies into building up Glenveagh – 40 square miles of Donegal's most rugged and inaccessible land. Over the following years the estate changed hands more than once and it was eventually bought by an Irish American, Henry McIlhenny, a descendant of a family evicted from the same area. In 1974 McIlhenny sold it to the Irish government and now, with its castle, gardens, and waterfalls, its woods clad in rowan and pine, and its hills covered with rhododendron, Glenveagh, returned to the safe-keeping of the Irish people, is the country's largest and most spectacular National Park.

But the Irish countryside would be nothing without its inhabitants. At first they may take a bit of finding, for the countryside is sparsely populated and the small, one-storied houses have a way of hiding from view behind trees and banks. Going up a narrow road, a boreen so little used that grass grows in the middle, not a house is in sight, though through the bushes you can see the ruins of many a poor old farmhouse, long since abandoned and now used as a byre for the cows. Over the hill comes a solitary figure, a man on a creaking, upright pushbike. Tied to the handlebars is his coat – for it will surely rain – and tied to the back carrier is a brown-paper parcel. He has been into the town on his errands – half a stone of potatoes, a sliced pan, a bag of porridge, a pound of rashers, some Galtee cheese and a couple of batteries for the wireless. The man pedals on up the next hill, turns on to the bog road

LEFT *Nature appears oblivious to the stonewall demarcations of what were once fields. These hills were once colonized by a burgeoning population, now the tide has turned.*

and slowly disappears from view. He is one of thousands of single men, living out a solitary life, cutting his own turf and hay, raising a couple of horses, fattening up a few cows, cultivating his lazy beds – the distinctive method of growing potatoes in these wet parts – and generally keeping himself to himself. He knows what goes on in the world, for he is an avid television viewer and he takes a special interest in programmes about the land, no matter of what country. He can name the longest river in the world and the highest mountain. He knows how many poles there are in a perch and how deep a fathom is. All this because he went to school in the days when these things were taught by rote and he has never forgotten them. He reads newspapers passed on to him by other people, which means that he is usually behind with what the rest of the world might consider to be of immediate importance. But what does that matter? When a man is used to waiting on the weather, such delays mean nothing. Time is the one thing he has plenty of. Once, about 20 years ago, he thought of marrying but you cannot have two women running one house, and his mother (he was her youngest and white-haired boy) lingered on so long that the other woman, seeing her child-bearing years slip away,

went off and married someone else.

The same fate will not befall his 22-year-old nephew, who, brought up in the same townland as his uncle, has already visited relatives in Canada and Australia. He has returned to help his father run the farm, commuting between the quiet of the small, slate-roofed farmhouse and the shrieking gales of the North Sea, where he works on one of the huge deep-sea trawlers, earning enough money there to keep him going for a few months at a time. His sister went off to England to train as a nurse. Now she comes home every year to join in the merriment of haymaking, for summer is the best time to be home. There are dances and discos, few of which start up before eleven at night and none of which finish before two in the morning. Every pub worth its salt has a dance floor, however small, and the streets outside are filled every summer night with the singing of sentimental ballads or the ever-popular country and western music. Depending on where you find yourself, a singer will be extolling the virtues of that very place, for every town and village has its own song, – 'The Star of County Down'. 'Limerick, you're a lady', or 'The Blue Hills of Antrim'. You may even hear the one which, years ago, took

everyone by surprise by becoming England's number one rec- ord for a day: 'I'm takin' the first puff-puff to Ballyjamesduff'.

Summer is the time for angling festivals and the grandly named regattas – wild, rowdy affairs where hardy men row against each other in big, heavy boats. It is also the time for music festivals – the 'fleadh ceoil' and the 'feiseanna' – when all the best traditional music from the land of music itself can be heard. Each year the roads into Letterkenny and Listowel are thronged with musicians and music-lovers, come to dance, sing and drink together for one glorious weekend.

And then there are the big fairs: West Kerry's annual Puck Fair, dating back to the 13th century and held in August, when a garlanded billy goat presides over a three-day riot of dancing and singing; the Ballinasloe Sheep and Cattle Fair, held in mid- October as in the old days, when the drovers needed time to get their stock up to Dublin and across the Irish Sea for the big English fairs held round about Hallowe'en; and the last of the great Connemara horse fairs, the Maam Cross Fair, stretching out three miles along each road of the four crossroads, with its big dance, the Bogman's Ball, to round off the festivities. On sale at the Maam Cross Fair are the tough little ponies from Connemara. So brave and hardy have they proved that they have been sent out to the tiny, mountainous African Kingdom of Lesotho as part of Ireland's Development Cooperation Programme there.

But it is not only for the fairs that country people gather together. There are wakes and funerals as well – the occasions so popular with MacNamara's Band – and the long line of cars following behind a hearse, perhaps a hundred of them, bears witness to the respect still afforded to the dead and the bereaved. Not that death is always taken too seriously by the Irish; they are, after all, a Celtic people, fascinated rather than terrified by the goings on of the Underworld. Death is seen as a part of life, as natural as the dying off of the year. There is not a lot to be done about it except take a few hours off work to show your respect – and maybe do a few other things as well, for it is not every day that you make the journey into the main town of the county.

After the death of a relative who lived in the local town, a good 20 miles away, a young man came into the bar, dressed up in his solemn suit, dispensing philosophy as freely as drink. 'I'll tell you what I did,' he said, loosening his tie and ordering a round. 'I was a tied for time, do you see, so I said to meself, sure God forgive me, I'll go to the barber's, the dispensary and the wake – all in the one stride.'

TOP LEFT *Kinsale, County Cork; the Irish poet Lennox Robinson once described how mackerel and herring boats crowded into the bay so tightly that one could 'walk the whole way from deck to deck' without ever touching the pier.*

LEFT *Changing weather in County Wexford; the sea has been providing the fishermen of Wexford with a living since about the year 850.*

TOP *Rosse's Point in County Sligo, where the poet W B Yeats spent many school holidays.*

ABOVE *Wexford: Viking, Norman, Welsh, Flemish and English soldiers all passed through this ancient gateway into Ireland.*

RIGHT AND ABOVE RIGHT *The Burren, County Clare, called by one geographer 'Ireland's botanical museum' is technically a 'karst', or limestone desert, a haven for exotic Alpine, Mediterranean and American flora.*

OPPOSITE AND LEFT The cliffs of Moher extend for some five miles along the Clare coastline; wind erosion has sloped the earth gently away on the inland side. The cliffs present a sheer wall of carboniferous limestone over 600 feet high.

ABOVE AND RIGHT Haystacks near Lisdoonvarna, County Clare, where there is an annual cultural festival with music and poetry. The stacks must be netted to keep them from being blown away.

24

ABOVE LEFT *Near New Ross, County Wexford; note the modern bungalow in the shadow of the church. In Ireland, there is (as yet) no premium on land for building, so single storey housing is common.*

ABOVE *County Kerry stretches out into the Atlantic, as the most westerly part of Europe; in the distance the Magillycuddy's reeks, a range of mountains just west of Killarney.*

LEFT AND OPPOSITE, ABOVE *Kerry developed early as a tourist attraction and the circular road, round the mountains, along the coast and past the lakes, taken by thousands of visitors in open carriages, or 'jaunting cars', became known as the Ring of Kerry.*

BELOW *Gallarus Oratory, County Kerry. One of the most perfect examples of the early Christian churches, it is thought to have been built some time in the eighth century. Built with dry stones, its interior is fifteen feet high and eight feet wide.*

BELOW LEFT *Dumbrody Abbey, near New Ross, County Wexford; built in 1182 by the monks of St Mary's Abbey, Dublin, the abbey had right of sanctuary and became known as the Monastery of St Mary the Refuge. The last Abbot was Alexander Devereux, who was made Bishop of Ferns in 1537.*

26

A journey along the southern coast, from Bantry Bay in the south west, where the sea has invaded the river valley between Dursey Island and Sheeps Head (RIGHT), via the fishing port of Kinsale, County Cork (ABOVE, TOP, AND ABOVE RIGHT), to the more sheltered farms of County Waterford (OPPOSITE, ABOVE); arable land and pasture cover nearly 70 per cent of Ireland.

FAR RIGHT Granard fort, County Longford: a classic motte – reputed to be the largest in Ireland – built by the Normans as part of their conquest of the area in the twelfth century. This earthworks would have originally been crowned by a wooden or stone fortification when it was first built by Hugh de Lacy in 1191.

28

LEFT AND BOTTOM LEFT *Near Kylemore, County Galway; close by stands the famous Kylemore abbey, the last of the castle houses to be built in Ireland. It was constructed by a Liverpool merchant in 1860 and is now occupied by a religious order.*

RIGHT *Connemara; it is difficult to believe looking at this breathtaking emptiness that for centuries much of the west suffered from overpopulation, as the English colonists drove the Catholics from the rich eastern lands after Cromwell's bloody campaigns.*

30

RIGHT One is never very far from water in Ireland. The central lowlands abound with quiet lakes, ideal for fishing. Salmon are to be found in the west.

OPPOSITE, ABOVE A calm sea at Clifden, Connemara; looking toward the twelve Pins, or Bens, part of the natural fortification of weathered mountains which protect the northern flank of the area.

OPPOSITE, BELOW A curiously self-conscious petrification of a living history at Bunratty Folk Museum, County Clare; in Ireland there is no need to visit a museum to see peat or a cottage: although most peat is now machine-dug, and this cottage clearly represents the fear that the old rural way of life is always under threat.

THE
CHURCH

Shrines like this were constructed in many
rural areas during the 1950s when religious
enthusiasm appeared to be on the increase.

34

In the summer of 1979, Pope John Paul 11 visited Ireland. The visit turned into a powerful display by the Irish people of their deep commitment to Roman Catholicism. At Drogheda, at Limerick, at Knock and elsewhere the extraordinary enthusiasm shown by people of all ages and backgrounds proved that de Valera's observation was still relevant in the modern world.

It is impossible to understand Irishness without understanding the significance of Roman Catholicism. As recently as 1986 the majority of Irish people voted in favour of a constitutional ban on divorce. Secularism might be the norm in most of Europe, but in Ireland personal morality is still firmly tied to the views of the Roman Catholic hierarchy.

In order to explain the strength of the relationship between religion and nationality in Ireland, it is necessary to go back many centuries. The roots of Christianity in Ireland can be traced to the arrival of St Patrick in the year 432. The previously pagan Irish people threw themselves into the new religion with a passion that few, if any, countries have been able to rival. The power of Christianity transformed the Gaelic culture and the pagan rites of Ireland were eventually driven out of the country altogether. St Patrick, the patron saint of Ireland, is commemorated by a giant statue on the hills of Tara.

By the sixth century, Christianity had spread throughout almost all of Ireland. In its forms and organization the Irish church was monastic. For three centuries the life of the monasteries dominated the countryside. Remnants of this great period exist today throughout Ireland. At Glendalough in the Wicklow hills there remains a round tower, a church and a burial place. On the island of Skellig Michael, off the county of Kerry, a church and surrounding beehive-like buildings have survived, precariously placed 700 feet above the sea.

Monasteries were centres of learning as well as faith. Records of the scholarship of this period have thankfully been pre-

BELOW RIGHT *The Pope's visit to Ireland in 1979 was a triumphant affirmation of the country's unbroken adherence to the Roman Catholic Church.*

OPPOSITE, ABOVE *The Catholic church of SS Peter and Paul, Athlone, County Westmeath, built in 1937.*

OPPOSITE, BELOW *Timealogue Abbey in County Cork is a Franciscan Friary established in 1240. It was sacked by English troops in 1642, but extensive ruins survive.*

served. One such item is the *Book of Durrow*, which is a seventh-century transcription of the gospels. Most famous of all works from this period is the glorious *Book of Kells*. A 19th-century scholar of this remarkable illuminated manuscript, J.O. Westwood, described it as 'the most beautiful book in the world'. No one who has seen it could honestly disagree. The origin of this late eighth-century gospel work is uncertain. It is normally associated with Kells in County Meath, but work on it may well have started by Columban monks on the island of Iona. The book has gained fame for the intricacy of its illustrations and for its sheer size. There are 680 quarto pages covering the four gospels without any duplication of the illuminations, which display an infinite variety of colour, design and imagery. The Book of Kells is safely housed in Trinity College, Dublin. No visitor to Ireland should miss it.

The golden period of Gaelic, Christian Ireland came to an end with the arrival of Norman longboats in 1169. The invasion did not, however, fundamentally alter the ideological strength of the Christian religion in Ireland. What was far more significant was the failure of the Protestant Reformation of the 16th century to make any inroads into Ireland. The Irish remained steadfast in their support for the Roman wing of Christianity. In the context of European politics, this was highly significant, since Protestant England and Scotland found themselves surrounded by Roman Catholic France, Spain and Ireland. The fear that Ireland might be used as a backdoor for the invasion of

England was recurrent in government circles in London from the 16th century onward.

The response of the British state was two-fold. First, there was an attempt to plant Protestants in Ireland in order to introduce into the country a population who were loyal to Protestant Great Britain. This plantation occurred in the 17th century; it was only really successful in the north-east of the country, in parts of the province of Ulster. The second strategy was to nullify the power of the Catholics. A series of penal laws, enacted between 1695 and 1705, barred Catholics from purchasing land owned by Protestants, from holding public office, from voting and from joining the army.

The impact of this severe 'penal code' on the relationship between the people and their faith was crucial. There was a clear identity in the minds of ordinary people between being Irish, being Catholic and being persecuted. When people resisted the penal laws, they did so as Irish Catholics. As Sean O'Faioloain has written, 'religion began to be identified with patriotic resistance'. Roman Catholicism gave to Irish men and women their sense of national identity. Remnants of this period survive today. In some areas the local 'mass rock', where the local priest would say mass, still stands.

Most of the penal laws had disappeared from the statute book by the end of the 18th century. One critical disability, however, remained. Despite the fact that from the Union of Great Britain and Ireland in 1801 onwards the Irish sent members of parliament to Westminster (the parliament of Dublin was abolished by the Act of Union), Roman Catholics, who counted for 80 per cent of the Irish population, were banned from Parliament. The campaign against this injustice was led by Daniel O'Connell, backed by his massively supported organisation of the peasantry, the Catholic Association. In 1829 the British government capitulated. By the act of Catholic Emancipation Roman Catholics became eligible to sit in parliament. O'Connell's campaign had helped to strengthen the fusion of Irishness and Roman Catholicism.

The mould of Irish national life was now set. The chief distinction between being Irish and being British was one's religion, the Irish language having been largely destroyed by Great Britain by the mid-19th century. The rapport between church and people was greatly enhanced by the somewhat democratic nature of the church. The hierarchy was neither distant nor oppressive and the priesthood was drawn from all sections of the community. The simple nature of Irish Catholicism was suited to a rural, peasant society. As Sir Horace

36

The origins of the magnificent book have never been totally authenticated. However the consensus is that it can be traced to the Irish monastery of St Columb Cille on the Island of Iona off the western coast of Scotland, at the end of the seventh and the beginning of the eighth century. The murderous raids of the Vikings were finally to make the continuation of monastic life a physical impossibility. In 806 for example, some 68 monks were killed. Land was given to the abbott Cellach at Kells in county Meath, and a new Monastery was built. The book was almost certainly one of the artefacts carried back across the sea to Kells. We can all be very thankful that the Viking raiders were both pagan and illiterate and therefore had no interest in this most beautiful of all books. The book was now housed in what has become known as Colum Cille's house at Kells. It was later moved to Trinity College, Dublin.

The Irish monk or monks responsible for the book are unknown, but as one writer observed, "he might have been

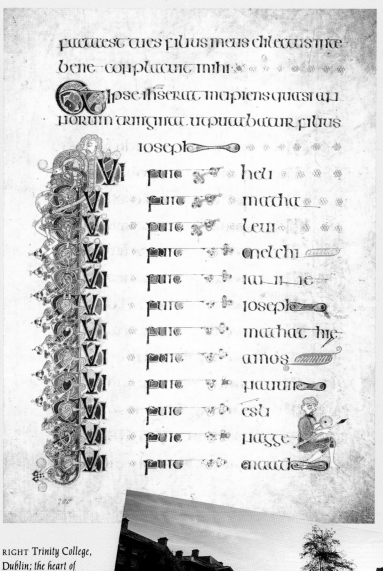

another Michaelangelo", such is the diversity and the richness of this work. It remains perhaps the most salient reminder that, far from being the land of a backward and uncultured people, ancient Ireland contained elements of high culture to rival the best of Europe.

FAR LEFT *The symbols of the Four Evangelists from St Matthew's Gospel (folio 27v).*

LEFT *The Virgin and Child (folio 7v).*

ABOVE *'The Birth of Christ' Chi-Rho page from St Matthew's Gospel (folio 34r).*

ABOVE RIGHT *Example of illuminated uncial, and half-uncial lettering of the Latin text.*

RIGHT *Trinity College, Dublin; the heart of Protestant Ascendacy Ireland and home of the Book of Kells.*

Plunkett remarked at the time, 'in no other country ... is religion so dominant an element in the daily life as in Ireland'.

The centre of training for the Irish priesthood was the seminary at Maynooth in County Kildare. Spreading out from this institution were thousands of young men, who were to form the backbone of missionary work for the Roman Catholic church internationally throughout the 19th and 20th centuries. An ex-student reminisced about Maynooth in 1937: 'In this place of memories, one is open to many fancies. To see the oak stalls in the college chapel, darkening a little with the years, is to think of all who have been students there before my time and since. With no effort I can slip from the moorings of past and present, and see in this moment all rolled into one. The slowly moving lines of priests down through the college chapel is never ending; it goes into the four provinces of Ireland; it crosses the seas into neighbouring England and Scotland, and the greater seas into the Americas and Australia and Africa and China; it covers the whole earth.'

Ireland's greatest contribution to Roman Catholicism was this seemingly never-ending supply of priests who travelled the world and spread the faith. This missionary activity gave Ireland an international significance. Here was a small country, which had been subjected to all kinds of repression, showing that in one activity it could lead the world. National pride swelled in 1932, when the Eucharistic Congress was held in Dublin. Terence Browne described the event: 'There were special candelit masses held in the Phoenix Park ... Four thousand were received at a state reception in St Patrick's Hall in Dublin Castle and 20,000 people attended a garden party in the grounds of Blackrock college at the invitation of the Irish hierarchy. The week culminated with a mass in the Phoenix Park where a crowd of over a million people heard John McCormack sing Franck's *Panis Angelicus* and a papal message broadcast. For a moment Dublin must have seemed the centre of Christendom.'

Following the partition of Ireland in 1921, the new state that developed was in all real senses a Roman Catholic state. It was not just, as the 1926 census showed, that 92.6% of the population was Catholic. It was also that the very ethos of the new independent territory was fusion of Catholicism and nationalism. The 1937 constitution, written by Eamon de Valera, identified the theocratic nature of Ireland. It recognised 'the special position of the Holy Catholic, Apostolic and Roman Church' and introduced a constitutional ban on divorce. Opposition to this was not widespread.

In the new society there was a definite attempt by the

clergy to impose a uniform level of behaviour. Catholic morality was supposed to permeate every aspect of daily life. Witness the infamous pastoral message which was read out in churches four times a year from the 1920s: 'The danger to purity comes from pictures and papers and drink. But it comes more from the keeping of improper company than from any other cause. And there is no worse fermenter of this great evil than the dancing hall. The occasions of sin and sin itself are the attendance of night dances in particular. There may be and are exceptions but these are remarkably few. To say nothing of the special danger of drink, imported dances of an evil kind, the surroundings of the dancing hall, withdrawals from the hall for intervals and the dark ways home have been the destruction of virtue in every part of Ireland.' Some Irish Catholics will have

OPPOSITE *This cross is all that remains of the monastery founded by St Columba in the sixth century at Cuildrere, near Drumcliffe, County Sligo. The great dispute between St Culumba and St Finian about the ownership of a book occurred here. In the ensuing war between the kingdoms supporting the respective saints, some 3,000 were slain and St Columba was exiled to Scotland.*
ABOVE LEFT *Plague cross; little crosses like this remembering the Irish victims of wars, famines and plagues can be found in many unexpected rural settings.*
ABOVE RIGHT *A beautiful setting for a church in the vale of Avoca, County Wicklow.*

had the pleasure of hearing this message some 200 times, read to them in what were known as 'trousers churches' - men on one side, women on the other. The often told story of the Irish priest who put courting couples asunder with a blackthorn stick was not entirely legendary!

In the last 25 years Ireland has gone through fundamental internal changes which have affected the relationship between clergy and people. Down to the early 1960s Ireland was an isolated island off the west coast of Europe. Its geographical isolation was accentuated by the economic policies of successive governments since the 1930s, policies of protectionism and self-development. The great social, economic and cultural changes that had begun to sweep through Europe in the aftermath of the World War II had little impact on Ireland. The strong influence of the priest, particularly in the rural areas, remained. Ireland did, however, begin to change in the 1960s. One important catalyst of this change was television, the most powerful of all media, able to permeate Irish society with outside cultural influences in a way not experienced before. By the mid-1960s there were some 348,000 television sets in Ireland. 'Put crudely,' David Harkness has written, 'the Irish people now had a window on the world never before open to them; and that window opened on a strange and exciting vista which neither state nor church authorities could any longer hide from gaze.'

The TV culture was dominated by Anglo-Irish values – secular, challenging, often permissive. It represented a fundamental threat to the cultural ethos of Ireland. It was not just the new dramas which represented a challenge; there were also the documentaries. Leading members of the church found themselves having to defend their stance on a whole range of issues in front of an interviewer or audience who treated them with a lack of deference which was a shock to the system. The most important programme was the celebrated 'Late, Late Show', hosted by the inimitable Gay Byrne. Each Saturday night this chat show would discuss issues which had previously been treated as taboo. In their sitting rooms at home, Irish men and women were now confronted by the open discussion of questions such as contraception, abortion, homosexuality and celibacy. As one commentator observed, 'what at first seemed blasphemous or obscene very soon was taken to the heart of the viewing public as ordinary tea-time chat'.

Such an opening-up of discussion made a nonsense of some of the restrictions which existed. Censorship of books and films could not survive the changes that were manifesting themselves in the Irish consciousness. In 1967 the Minister of Justice passed legislation which led to the unbanning of more than 5,000 books. It was clear that the state could not ignore the reality of the new Ireland. But what of the church?

Catholicism on a global scale was, in fact, going through some of its most profound changes since the Reformation. Under the papacy of John XXIII, the second Vatican council (1962 to 1965) wrought truly revolutionary effects on many aspects of Roman Catholicism. The Latin mass was abolished and the replacement of the 'blessed mutter' of the ancient language by modern English had a demystifying effect. Many other changes were introduced: the abandonment of a number of feast days, the ending of the ban on meat on Friday, the decree that mass should now be said with the priest facing his congregation and the promise that the church would hence-

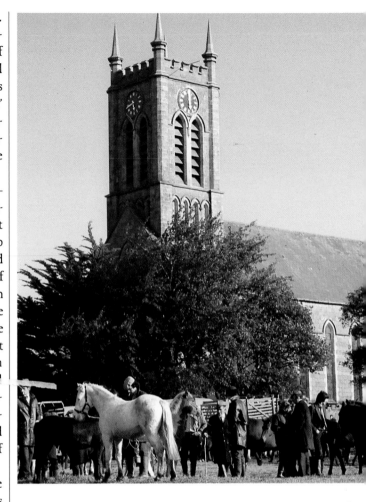

forth act and talk in a far more ecumenical fashion.

How would the church in Ireland react to this? Archbishop McQuaid of Dublin had no doubts whatsoever. As he landed at Dublin Airport on his return from Vatican 11, he told his countrymen 'no change will be allowed to disturb the tenor of your Christian lives'. Yet some change had to come and reforms began to filter through the system. In Dublin it had been decreed by the hierarchy that it was a mortal sin for any student to attend the Protestant university, Trinity College, Dublin. Catholics were to attend the other Dublin university, University College; in 1970 it was decreed that they were free to go to whichever they wished. Small though the change may appear, symbolically it was very important.

The challenge facing the church in Ireland was visible in a set of statistics: the steep decline in the number of men taking up a priestly vocation. By 1972 the number being ordained was down

• THE ROCK OF CASHEL •

ABOVE RIGHT *The Rock of Cashel in County Tipperary is the seat of the former Munster kings of Ireland. The huge 13th century cathedral that now crowns the rock is dedicated to 'God, Saint Patrick and Saint Ailbhe'.*

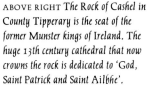

by 50 per cent from the 1950s. Important changes within the population were also proving a challenge for the Church. Ever since the Famine, Ireland's population had stagnated. The major cause of this was not size of family, which remained high, but the continuing fact of mass emigration. With job opportunities limited, it was commonplace for men to travel abroad in search of work. by the 1970s, however, the tide was beginning to turn. Emigration declined. The new prosperity which derived from Ireland's membership of the EEC and high unemployment in Great Britain made emigration less appealing. The population of Ireland began to grow for the first time since the famine, leaving Ireland the youngest population in Europe. Half the people were under the age of 25.

A young population who could not remember the Latin mass, could not remember the old days, was not going to accept the authority of the church. Pressure began to mount on a whole range of issues. Demands for legislation on family planning and divorce grew in strength. Opinion polls seemed to show that the church was lagging behind the consciousness of the population as a whole and the young in particular. Matters came to a head in 1986 when a referendum on divorce was held. The opinion polls, the media and most impartial observers were united in the belief that the result would be a clear vote in favour of removing from the constitution the section prohibiting divorce. How wrong they all were! When the results came in, it was clear that the country had voted in a very different way. By a majority of two to one, the people decided that the ban on divorce should remain. In that remarkable vote lies the evidence, if evidence be needed, that Roman Catholicism and its moral legacy are too deeply engrained in the Irish mind, too powerfully connected with the Irish people's sense of who they are, to crumble in a generation.

During the height of the land agitation in 1879, an apparition of the Virgin Mary appeared in the village of Knock, County Galway. Since then the village has become an important place of pilgrimage for people from all over Ireland; and more recently, after a long campaign, the government provided funds for an international airport to serve the shrine.

44

RIGHT *The Holy Trinity Church, Cork; building began in 1832, and the spire was completed in 1890. The church was restored to full Gothic splendour in 1982.*

BELOW RIGHT *Religious memorabilia on display at Knock shrine.*

FAR RIGHT *Attitudes to death mark off the Irish from many of their British and European neighbours. Wakes have always been a noted part of Irish life; and reference to 'the family plot' is as likely to refer to the graveyard as to any piece of real estate.*

Houses
and
Towns

The Four Courts, Dublin; a creation of the
Enlightenment and the Protestant
Ascendancy. Built by James Gandon
between 1780 and 1790, they were burnt
down in 1921 during the war of
independence, but have since been sensitively
restored.

I will arise and go now, and go to Innisfree,
And a small cabin build there, of clay and wattles made:
Nine bean-rows will I have there, a hive for the honey-bee,
And live alone in the bee-loud glade.

W B YEATS

The idea of an Irish house brings to mind a little whitewashed cabin with its half door and yellow thatch gleaming in the slanting sunshine. It is a picture reinforced by a thousand tourist advertisements and a score of Hollywood movies. Constructed of local materials – stone along the harsh Atlantic seaboard, mud and timber in the flat bogland and in the heavy claylands of the east – its familiar form and local colour blended easily into the Irish landscape.

In size and external form the traditional thatched house appears similar throughout the country. But there are a number of regional variations. Hip-roof houses with a central hearth predominate in the south-east, while gables and gable chimneys are more common in the west and north-east. In appearance these houses, together with the maze of stone walls and untamed hedges, have struck many observers as untidy and as evidence of a want of skill on the part of the inhabitants. Stacks of hay, turf and potatoes, collected in heaps around the houses, reinforced this impression. This may have been a ploy to deceive land agents, who might put rents up if they saw any real improvement. But it is more likely to have been the result of the relaxed tempo of peasant life, what William Carleton termed the 'Paddy-go-easy' attitudes of country life. Visiting agriculturists of the 19th century disapproved, but to contemporary tourists this quiet world presents a scene of charm and relaxation a long way from the rush of city life.

The very simplicity of these little houses meant that they could be erected by a few neighbours over a couple of weeks, and since most of the materials (with the exception of roofing timbers) were plentiful, they appeared everywhere. They could be found in groups by a crossroads, as a continuous line of habitations facing the street in the outskirts of towns, grouped higgledy-piggledy in rural settlements (in the north and west of Ireland) or, most common of all, gable end to the road in the open countryside.

In form these houses have a long history and resemble primitive houses in many lands. Excavations in Louch Gur, County Limerick, have revealed house structures some 4,000 years old in which one can see the origins of the thatched house. In the 17th century the Great O'Neill lived in a clay-walled, straw-covered hall, and many other Irish chiefs retained similar structures long after they had begun to build well-fortified, stone-tower houses for sleeping and defence. Thatched houses were well insulated against the elements –

LEFT *This pub was clearly once a farmhouse, for these types of half-doors were commonly installed as a means of keeping out hens and other farm animals, while allowing light and air in on a summer's day.*

RIGHT *Hip-roof thatched cottages – a style common in the south east – near Wicklow. In County Wicklow, 'the tired worker, the overtaxed, the student . . . many regain elasticity for the mind, tone for the nervous system, and restoration of bodily vigour.' (Richard Lovett, Irish Pictures, 1888). Both cottages however, if examined closely, reveal signs of modernization: the cottage above has had some kind of loft conversion, while the one below has been altered so radically that the roof almost seems to belong to another house.*

warm in winter and cool in summer. But they offered no protection to the Gaelic chiefs, during times of disturbance, against cannon and arson.

None of the great thatched dwellings from the 17th century still exist. Timberframe, mud and thatch have a comparatively short life in the humidity of the Irish climate. They require perpetual renewal and rebuilding; current Irish domestic housing has been the creation of the last few hundred years and most dwellings date from the post-Famine period.

In spite of their often disorderly appearance, the old houses were neither so simple nor so easily built as their form might suggest. Generations of refinements and familiarity with local materials called a variety of skills into existence. Stone foundations had first to be laid, on which the mixture of damp clay and rushes was piled, dried and cut in a series of layers to form the house walls. The base of each wall had to be broad enough so that, as it tapered away towards the top, it was still sufficiently solid and strong to carry the weight of the roof timbers and thatch. Windows and doors were then cut into the walls. In the west the thatch has to be secured by ropes weighed with stones against the Atlantic gales. Chimneys were constructed to provide for cooking needs while avoiding the risk of allowing the dry, combustible thatch to catch fire. Chimneys were a comparatively late development. Most 18th-century peasant cottages simply allowed the smoke to blow out through the doors or a smoke hole in the roof. Many people were happy to receive the extra warmth gained from retaining the smoke, regardless of the irritation to their eyes.

At its best the traditional house was very comfortable. Unfortunately, during the period of rapid population growth in the late 18th century standards fell and a rapid deterioration in house-building took place. Skills were no longer transmitted from one generation to the next and raw materials, particularly roofing timbers, became scarce as the land was stripped of trees for fuel. The result was crude shelters, thrown together against embankments or along the sides of roads. Comfort was lost as these habitations came more and more to resemble the landscape out of which they sprang – mere sods, branches and clumps of rushes unfashioned by plan or tradition. They multiplied with every subdivision of farm plots so that, in the words of the old Irish saw 'it was impossible to cross a ditch without falling down a chimney'.

The mid-19th century Famine was primarily the tragedy of the small farmers and the peasantry and many of the deaths were caused as much by inadequacy of shelter as from lack of

food. 1847 was not only the year when the potato crop failed; it was also the coldest in living memory. Many families in makeshift housing died from cold or from diseases related to the effects of dampness and lack of shelter.

Just as post-Famine society moved away from reliance on potatoes as the chief source of food, so, too, there was a virtual revolution in Irish housing. In 1841, one-roomed, mud cabins made up the largest proportion of the housing stock. In not a single county did this type of dwelling account for less than 20 per cent of the total housing – and in some it was well over 60 per cent. By 1891 the mud cabins had virtually disappeared; only in Kerry and Limerick did they still account for six to eight per cent. Despite failed harvests, the land war and continued poverty among the labouring classes, the last quarter of the 19th century was, for the majority of the agricultural population, a period of rising expectations and improved conditions. In housing it was a time of reconstruction: the replacement of thatch by slate, the raising of many country houses by an extra storey, and a programme of council building of slated cottages for the rural labourers.

These housing changes reflected important changes in the Irish countryside. Emigration reduced the population; farms were consolidated as adjoining holdings were combined through arranged marriages and land purchase; and the terms of land tenure changed from rent to peasant proprietorship. Marriage patterns changed, too. Most farmers married later, if they married at all, and the numbers of the unmarried – bachelors and spinsters, nuns and priests – increased rapidly, so that Irish life began to take on the character with which we are still familiar. The house with the couple of fields became the basic social and production unit. Woman's role became in-

FAR LEFT *News international, national and provincial: note the lead story of* The Cork Examiner.

ABOVE LEFT *Not all murals are political; this one in Westport, County Mayo, has a suitable theme for a coastal town and is quite an effective* trompe-l'oeil.

Most shops are brightly painted like these in Hillsborough, County Down (ABOVE AND RIGHT) *and Bantry, County Cork* (BELOW RIGHT) *– to attract the eye of a potential customer, naturally – but also perhaps simply as a reaction to the grey weather. Craft shops now rely on the tourist trade, but basket and cloth weaving, and the other skills of a poor, pre-industrial society, were flourishing for centuries before the first intrepid traveller went west.*

creasingly that of housewife and mother while the man's domain became the fields and bog. Women may previously have played a greater role in field work, particularly before the introduction of the horse plough; and they worked as domestic earners before the market for homespun textiles declined with the introduction of factory goods.

As the house grew, it became both a workshop for butter-making, spinning, cooking and all the chores connected with running a farm, and more the social focus of family life. Seats by the big, open chimney provided a snug corner for the ill or the very old; and the whole room was oriented towards the fire-place. Other features of the room were the dresser and the broad, scrubbed table where the whole family – and at harvest and sowing time, the men from several farms round – gathered for their meals. It comprised the social world of family and community, both a place of work and, in the evenings, one of entertainment where neighbours chatted, danced and played cards.

The rural community of the 19th century relied for its services on neighbouring towns. The towns themselves were

52

• SHOPFRONTS •

Meticulously painted shop fronts in Kilkenny, (historically the city of rich merchants), Westport (right) and Bunratty (below right); individual retailers are embattled in Ireland, as are small shopkeepers everywhere, confronted by the challenge of the supermarket, but by eliciting loyalty from their customers many have survived. Rosary beads alongside the tobacco; a world away from the shopping mall, and one of the delights of visiting the cities.

mainly the creation of the 16th-century transformation of Ireland. Before then Ireland had very few towns except for some ports established by the Normans in the 12th century. From the Tudor and Stuart conquest and plantation a new commercial elite emerged, comprising Scots, English and those Gaelic and Old English who conformed to the newly established religion of Protestantism. They became known as 'the Ascendancy' and they conducted their affairs on the basis of a money economy: rent and the sale of agricultural produce from their tenants. Commercialism, previously a minor aspect of Irish life, now became its driving force. Magnificent houses were built on the profit from rents and towns grew up in which peasants could trade for cash. They brought their cattle and other produce there, sold them and paid their rents with the proceeds. Pastoralism was replaced by intensive tillage, which commanded higher export prices per acre and created greater revenue for the landlord. That was the basis of the great town and country-house building programme of the 18th century.

The big houses built by the Ascendancy became the focus of Irish upper-class life Armies of servants and builders managed the house and gardens. Hunts, balls, visits to spas and seasons in Dublin and London kept high society in a continual state of movement and excitement, much of it with a distinctly English flavour. But traditional Irish aspects could also be found in the faction fights, drinking sprees and love of conviviality which united landlords and tenants together in spite of the exploit-ative nature of much of their relationship and the violent pro-test offered by some agragarian organizations. As the size and importance of houses increased, so the social divide between the various classes opened up. Great avenues separated the land-lord from tenant; ante-chambers and hallways isolated the gen-tility of the noble family from the ne'er-do-well callers; and depressions around the edge of the houses prevented the ser-vants from spoiling the view between the drawing room and the lawns.

Unfortified houses, like that of Beaulieu in County Louth, completed in the 1660s, began a pattern of building which reached its climax just over a hundred years later. In common with British taste of the time they looked to the Italian Renaissance and classical principles for their style. Houses like Castletown, County Kildare, built in the 1720s, and Emo Park, Leix, built at the end of the century, are particularly fine examples of this trend. Wood-pannelled walls, stucco ceilings and symmetrical staircases gave a new elegance to interiors, while planned gardens, lawns, avenues and parks added to the

• AN OUTPOST OF PROGRESS •

Two images of Clifden, County Galway, and two very different ways of life; when John D'Arcy purchased an estate here in 1815, he proceeded to build a residence in the style of a Gothic castle. When this photograph of the house was taken in the 1860s or 1870s, it and the estate of more than 8,000 acres were in the possession of the Eyre family, who were of English origin. By then Clifden had grown from nothing to a town with its own constabulary barracks, a national school, a union workhouse, and three churches. The railway did not arrive until 1895, but there was a passenger and mail service to Galway operated from 1837 by the well-known firm of Charles Bianconi; two Bianconi cars are shown. These cars could carry six people on each side in considerable discomfort, and one more on the box seat by the driver, with their luggage piled in the middle. The bearded man on the right is probably the manager of the Clifden Bianconi station. An anonymous passenger in 1870 observed that 'the four horses were poorly shod, and the substratum of harness was made out with bits of cord, which, however, did not prevent the traces from frequently breaking.'

54

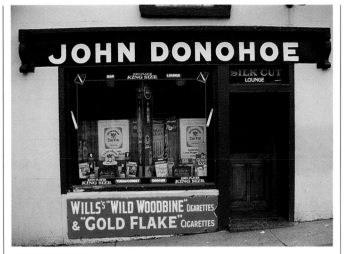

grandeur of the exterior setting. Powerscourt in County Wicklow, Rockingham House in County Roscommon, and Westport House, in County Mayo, have particularly graceful gardens.

A great number of towns were the creation of this new landlord class. Many, especially in the north, were, in fact, planned. They had a characteristically rectangular appearance, with a grid pattern of streets and a central square, or 'diamond', as it is known, in the centre. Apart from these features little remains of the early Irish towns. Youghal, a plantation town in County Cork, is distinctive in retaining one of the few complete 17th-century domestic buildings in the country – a group of alms houses in North Main Street. Most houses in Ireland date from the 18th century at the earliest and only the street pattern, the church perhaps, and the fortified castle date from earlier times.

Outside Ulster few towns had an industrial base. Most grew as a response to the commercial needs of the countryside; they were little more than centres where fairs were held and, in those established by the Ascendancy, settlements where the servants and country artisans who serviced the estate resided. With the growing prosperity of the comfortable classes there was less self-sufficiency and more dependence on bought goods. By the end of the 19th century the small town shop had come into being and the main street was composed of a string of retailers servicing the surrounding countryside.

The link between town and country carried trade along lines of family patronage, and as population fell, shopkeepers had to make greater and greater efforts to maintain the loyalty of their clientele. They needed to create relationships over and

LEFT *Many buildings in the west, like this pub in Westport, have an attractively squat, or shrunken appearance, as if huddled against the wind and rain.*

BELOW LEFT *A paucity of goods on display and an overall lack of sophistication in presentation in this grocer's is reminiscent of an earlier time.*

BELOW *Primary colours covering the brieze blocks in Dingle, County Kerry; the feel is Mediterranean, though the coastline of the Dingle peninsula is a far cry from that of gentler southern waters.*

above the cash nexus and this lent a peculiar intensity to small-town commercial life. Everything was done to provide the regular customer with his or her requirements; failure to do so in one small area might meant the loss of an entire family's trade to a rival. Special terms were always on offer: weekly credit, deferred payments and so on. Shopkeepers would buy their customer's butter, eggs and other farm produce in return for their custom. Drinks would be stood and Christmas boxes given in recognition of a family's loyalty during the year. The shopkeepers's life was a finely balanced one.

Competition between shops determined the dynamic of small-town life. As the Irish population declined from 1850 onwards, new businesses started up only at the expense of existing ones. The towns were little islands of fierce competition in a countryside where community feeling and neighbourliness were prized above all else. Successful shops exuded confidence. They displayed bright façades and extended their warehouses at the back. Success, whether it was due to favourable location or the owner's acumen or reputation, had the effect of transforming modest premises into General Providers. Expansion required the addition of a delivery truck and yardmen, which would in their turn make possible further expansion into hardware and ironmongery, timber and building materials.

As the number of customers increased specialist services became more economical, creating employment and increasing

RIGHT *Reginald's Tower, Waterford, is said to have been built by Reginald the Dane in 1003, but it is probably a thirteenth century Norman tower. The records show that in 1463 it was used as a mint and in the nineteenth century it served as a prison. Today it houses the City Museum.*

BELOW RIGHT *The stepped slate roofs at Hillsborough, County Down; North Down is an area of steep little hills like this one, called drumlins, deposits of glacial clay which make excellent arable farmland.*

BELOW *New Ross, County Wexford; the doubling up of grocer's shops as bars is a phenomenon peculiar to Ireland and few other countries in Europe.*

OPPOSITE, ABOVE *Communications, town and country; phoning home in Mulligan and a link with the outside world in the deserted hills of County Wexford.*

OPPOSITE, BELOW *O'Connell Street, Dublin: the O'Connell monument was unveiled on August 15, 1888.*

the influence of the shopkeeper in the surrounding countryside. The growth of one successful business drew trade to a town. Newsagents, butchers and drapery businesses blossomed in its wake. Customers moved from shops further down the street and sometimes from neighbouring towns and in this way old bonds carefully built up over a long period were broken and the trade of towns see-sawed as the centres of commercial gravity shifted. Strikingly, in recent decades, big towns have grown at the expense of small ones.

But towns were about more than trade. Successful shops were the conduits of change, of the new and the fashionable: they stocked the latest innovations, interesting people in new things and encouraging them to take risks with new products. Shopkeepers provided a lead in small-town life. Their political views were important and were reflected on the local council and even in the Irish parliament, the Dail. Although they comprised only three per cent of the population, they provided a third of all local councillors and a fifth of government ministers in the first 50 years of the new state. They encouraged revolution when their customers supported it – 20 per cent of those convicted by courts during the Land League crisis of the 1880s were shopkeepers – and frowned upon it when it threatened to disrupt their trade.

The larger towns became centres of administration, welfare and recreation in the early 19th century. (Only in Northern Ireland, Dublin and a few of the provincial towns was there sufficient industry to create the working-class enclaves so prevalent in English and Scottish cities.) The classical style of architecture which the Victorians favoured to express an administrative function provide many of these towns with the centrepiece. Carlow, Dundalk and Hillsborough each have fine court houses and others, like Naas, Sligo and Cavan, had impressive town halls. After 1867 and the establishment of the Royal Irish Constabulary most Irish towns had barracks, and a few, for instance Birr, Fermoy and Eniskillen, were garrison towns dominated by the military. The Poor Law Act of 1836 laid the foundations of a welfare programme and most of the larger towns had a workhouse built on the outskirts. These forbidding and feared institutions, like those in England, have since been converted to other more enlightened purposes: as hospitals and schools they form an important feature of the larger towns. There has also been an increase in recreational buildings – libraries, cinemas, swimming pools and dance halls forming a centre of interest and activity.

The growth of these services swelled the number of

workers and administrators in residential areas. Many of the new professionals – accountants, lawyers, vets, agricultural advisers – built impressive surburban bungalows in a variety of exotic styles, while converting older Georgian houses in the centre into offices. In the 1960s only 25 towns had more than 10,000 residents, but since then there has been a steady shift from smaller towns to larger.

Of all the 19th-century changes in Ireland the growth in church-building was the most wide-reaching and the most visible. By the end of the century almost every town had acquired a new Roman Catholic church, and many of the larger ones had fine gothic and classical cathedrals. St. Mary's Cathedral, Killarney, built in 1855, and St John's, Limerick, opened in 1861, provide examples of the new style of ecclesiastical building.

What one historian has called 'a devotional revolution' increased the number of clergy and nuns and the number of convents, church schools and hospitals grew accordingly. The Protestant Church of Ireland had a church-building programme, too, but as the numbers of Protestants of all denominations declined in southern Ireland in the 20th century, fewer new churches were required. Only in Ulster was there a comprehensive growth in the number of Presbyterian churches to match that of Catholic ones in the south.

The major Irish cities have had mixed fortunes. During the 18th century Dublin was the second city in the British empire and one of the ten major cities of Europe. As befitted such status, it was remodelled and its customs, university and parliament were housed in some of the finest buildings of the period. Visitors from London and abroad remarked on the superiority of Gandon's Customs House, the old Parliament building, the Four Courts and Trinity College. Yet within a few decades of their construction the city was stagnating, its trade declining and its industry eclipsed by the rapid industrial growth of Belfast in the north. In the 1820s Belfast had a population of some 37,000, compared with Dublin's 178,000. By 1911 Belfast had grown to 387,000 outstripping Dublin's 304,000. Belfast's success was based on thriving shipbuilding, engineering and linen industries, which attracted migrants from all over Ulster to its factories.

It is difficult to account for this reversal of fortune. The Act of Union of 1801, which removed the government of Ireland to London, has usually been blamed for Dublin's decline. But Dublin was not unique. It shared many similarities with London and Edinburgh: in each the industrial sector declined while the

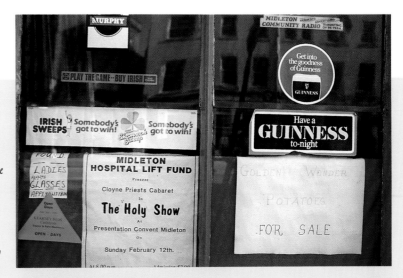

FAR LEFT The elegant and inviting interior of The Long Hall in Dublin city centre.

LEFT Tomasin's Bar is on the road to Dingle, County Kerry; business thrives on the busy road in this Gaeltacht area, both in the bar and in the craft shop attached.

BELOW LEFT Unlike Boyd's, several Irish liqueurs are still made, the most successful being Bailey's Irish Cream. O'Darby Irish Cream is made from whiskey and a touch of chocolate. A liqueur is defined as a spirit mixed with flavouring and containing at least 2.5 per cent sugar by volume; some Irishmen have been known to define it as a waste of good whiskey.

BELOW The delicate, muted colours of the stained glass in Ryan's Bar, Dublin.

TOP RIGHT Signs of a parochial community in Midleton, County Cork.

RIGHT Pub mirror advertising Paddy whiskey; sales of this brand are good in the home market, but lag behind Jameson abroad.

BELOW RIGHT The curious trompe-l'oeil painting on the wall of Dan Foley's has been reproduced as a post-card for years. 'It's an illusion': it is up to the visitor to decide just how apt that comment is, as a message to send home during a visit to this extraordinary country.

Irresistible invitations to a national pastime, in Glengariff, County Cork, Kilkenny, and Dublin (ABOVE, RIGHT AND MIDDLE).

FAR RIGHT *Some of the most unusual places turn out to be pubs. It is quite easy not to notice that you can get a drink here in Cork.*

food, light-engineering and printing sectors grew. Dublin's prosperity in the late 18th century was based on the production of luxury items and the supply of goods to the gentry who were building the Georgian squares on either side of the Liffey. With the growth of a mass market cities turned to the creation of a food-and-drinks industry. Guinness's Brewery was one of the outstanding successes. Unskilled labour engaged in casual docking and cartier work became the main source of employment for the Dubliner. With the retreat of the comfortable middle-classes to the suburbs, many of the fine streets deteriorated into ghettos for the impoverished. Other Irish cities – Cork, Galway, Limerick and Derry – all grew at a slow, steady pace which reflected their positions as the capitals of improving regions more than any industrial upsurge peculiar to themselves.

From 1921 until the outbreak of World War II Belfast was hit by a series of trade depressions. During some years, 1931 and 1938 for instance, as many as a quarter of the population were out of work. Shipbuilding and the linen industry were undergoing long-term contraction. In contrast Dublin showed a steady rate of growth after the creation of the new independent Ireland in 1921. Restored to its position as the seat of government, it grew as an administrative and commercial centre. Industry, too, diversified, reflecting the growing wealth and higher

expectations of the people; but a glance at the output of manufacturing firms indicates that it catered mainly for a home market. Light engineering, food-processing, brewing, distilling, textiles, footwear, biscuits, chocolate and jam manufacture contrasted with Belfast's export-led shipbuilding, aircraft and linen industries. By the 1960s Dublin's population had reached 660,000 and its suburbs had grown to embrace many of the surrounding smaller centres of population. Belfast's growth had been slower and its population stood at just over half a million.

The last 20 years have seen major changes in Irish town life. In the north, the Troubles have destroyed many of the working-class residential areas and caused a major movement of the population. In the Republic a rapid programme of rural industrialization has begun, with large incentives provided for international companies to invest in Ireland. Ultra-modern factories have been built, attracting people from other areas (including Northern Ireland and Great Britain). The changing composition of Ireland's population has affected not only the tone, but the orientation of town life. The average age of the population has fallen steeply: previously the most elderly in Europe, it is now the youngest and this has led to a rapid expansion of welfare, educational and recreational facilities.

In the 1980s there were signs that the pace of change in the

south had been too fast. The growth of the large cities, particularly Dublin, began to outstrip job opportunities: unemployment figures rose and emigration resumed. In Northern Ireland the problems which currently affect many British cities – the decline of manufacturing industries and the contraction in demand for unskilled labour taking place more rapidly than the creation of new industries – have been exacerbated by the continued shifts of the population along sectarian lines.

These factors have arrested the trends of the last few decades. Whether this is only a temporary suspension of the upward trends in population and urban growth, or a reversal to the more static society of the past, it is impossible to say, but there are many things that encourage hopeful prospects. The media, tourism and returning migrants have made the Irish people much more aware of life lived in other countries: the old attitudes of 'making do' with standards inherited from the past is no longer acceptable. There is a new pride in preserving the Irish heritage, and nowhere can this be seen better than in the new awareness of architecture. From the outcry over the proposed building of an office block on one of Dublin's historical Viking sites to the growth in publishing of books about Irish houses and towns, the signs are that every effort will be made to maintain the best of that inheritance.

Pubs in Mulligan and Galway; The diversity of buildings that make up Irish public houses will never cease to surprise and fascinate the visitor. Along the length and breadth of the country, there is an almost infinite variety of choice.

ABOVE *Bunratty Castle; this Norman castle is popular with tourists because of the traditional music provided for them by resident harpists and other musicians; despite existing quite openly purely for the tourist trade, the music is of a high standard.*

TOP RIGHT *Leinster House, the meeting place of the Irish parliament in Dublin. The American White House was modelled on this building.*

RIGHT *This magnificent mock-Elizabethan building stands on the shores of Lough Poolacappul. The limestone-faced granite construction is now a school supervised by Benedictine sisters.*

LEFT AND TOP LEFT *Ireland's most southerly city, Cork, a place of great history, of culture and rebellion. Its people see themselves as belonging first to Cork and only secondly to Ireland.*

ABOVE *The wealth accrued by the old Irish landlords can be clearly seen in this picture of Powerscourt in County Wicklow; built on 14,000 acres in the eighteenth century, the house is at the end of a mile-long avenue.*

PORTALS OF HISTORY

The renewal of Dublin was so complete that by 1800 there was very little to be seen that was more than a hundred years old. British and European architects were invited to Ireland by wealthy patrons. Some only stayed long enough to complete their commissions, but James Gandon arrived in 1781 and stayed for the rest of his life, designing the three major public buildings of Neo-Classical Dublin – the Four Courts, the Custom House and the Kings' Inns. He was a pupil of Sir William Chambers, who never visited Ireland, but designed the town house of Lord Charlemont, illustrated below (set back on the left), on the north side of Rutland Square. The square, (now Parnell Square) was laid out in the 1750s; it was then that stage-coaches began to run on the main thoroughfares. An attempt to alleviate the abysmal lot of the Dublin poor was made by Dr Bartholomew Mosse, who organized the Rotunda charity; income from a pleasure garden and assembly rooms in front of the square was given to the Rotunda Lying-In Hospital.

This was the first maternity hospital in the whole of the British isles.

Doors on the architectural soul of a city; Dublin was practically remodelled during the establishment of the Anglo-Irish Ascendancy; Palladio was the driving force, and colonnades, porticos and friezes began to appear along the banks of the Liffey. The overall effect of the façades was quite austere, the only ornamentation being wrought-iron balconies, fanlights over the doors, and the doors themselves, brightly painted and lacquered (then as now) to offset the granite and brick.

OPPOSITE, ABOVE Georgian influence in Hillsborough and Mulligan (RIGHT).

OPPOSITE, BELOW Saint Stephen's Green, Dublin, a Guinness bequest.

LEFT Flower seller, Dublin.

TOP Exterior Rococo tile, Dublin; a hint of the flamboyant Georgian stucco-work often to be found inside.

ABOVE Mural, Dublin; a city obsessed with itself.

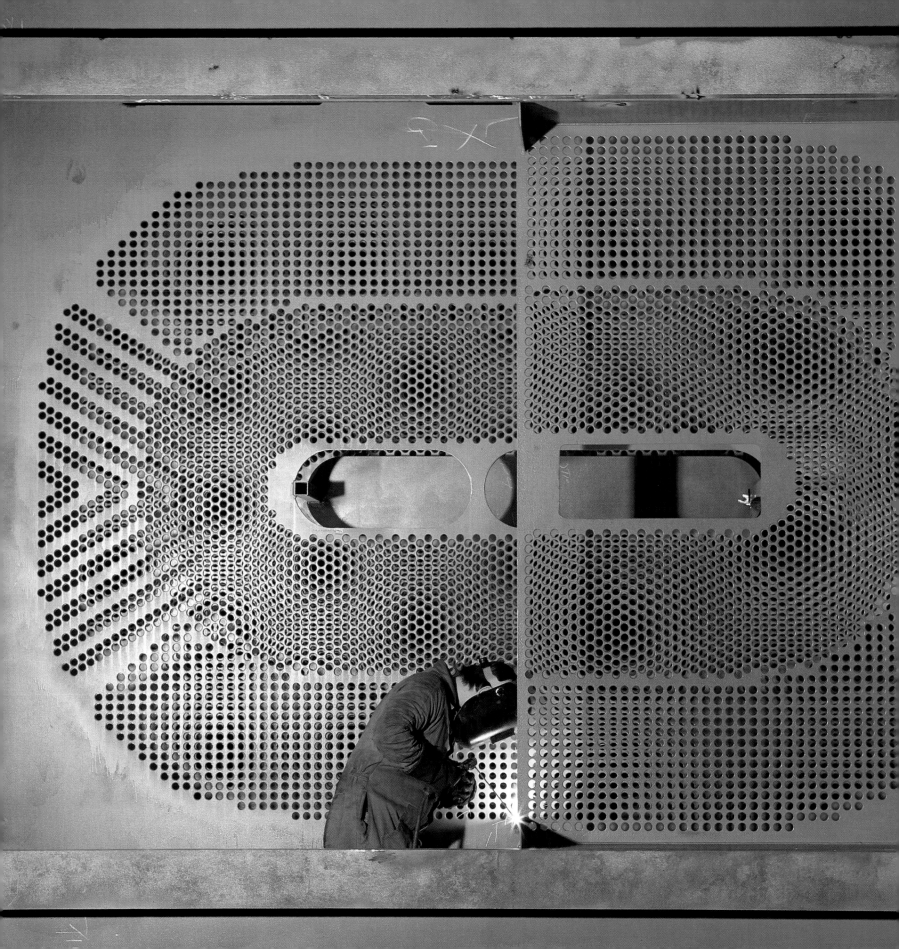

IRISH
INDUSTRY

The industrial future of Ireland? High-tech
multinationals, such as GEC Turbine
generators in Larne. They have become a
common feature of Irish industrial life in the
last twenty five years.

Though it does not accord well with the popular conception of Ireland as a traditionally agricultural country, industry has played an important part in the development of the Irish economy for at least two centuries. The era of peace in Ireland which followed the fall of the Stuart monarchy in 1689, after a century of incessant warfare, combined with world-wide increase in agricultural prosperity to stimulate the development of a wide range of industries. Wool and linen fabrics, glass, beer, whiskey, refined sugar and flour were some of the products from the hundreds of factories which sprang up throughout the country during these years. Many of these businesses depended on buoyant home demand; but Irish industry even then was heavily engaged in exports to Great Britain, the continent, North America and the British colonies. The harnessing of steam and water power was adopted as widely in Ireland as in Great Britain. Indeed, in the second half of the 18th century there was a substantial lobby in Great Britain against the proposal that Irish manufacturers should have free access to the British market. Much of the industrial progress of the 18th century was lost during the first half of the following century, when the economic cycle entered one of its long downturns. But the years after about 1890 saw a revival which lasted up to World War I. By the turn of the century, the net output of Irish industry was half as large as that of agriculture and half of that industrial output was exported. These were high ratios for any economy at the time so Ireland was a comparatively highly industrialized country.

Irish industry had one characteristic, however, which was to exercise an important influence on subsequent economic and political developments. Whereas in the 18th century Irish industry had been spread throughout the country, by 1900 it was heavily concentrated in the Belfast region in the north. The most outstanding example of this concentration was the ship-building industry, which comprised two Belfast companies, Harland and Wolff and Workman, Clark and Company. At the height of their pre-war success these two companies launched more than .25 million tons of shipping. The other major sector largely concentrated in the north was the linen spinning and weaving industry. Food, drink and tobacco manufacture, on the other hand, was more evenly divided between north and south.

The economic differences between the two parts of the country led to radically different views of the possible effect of

Drinking bitter stout rather than ale has long been the norm in Ireland: although foreign lagers have recently made some inroads into this valuable market.

independence. As the notion of ending the union between Great Britain and Ireland gained acceptance in the latter years of the 19th century and the beginning of the 20th, the northern population noted with alarm the economic objectives of the leaders of the independence movement, who, like their chief spokesman, Arthur Griffith, were from the south. They wished to use independence to impose tariffs on imports into the country. The country as a whole lacked enough industry to provide employment for the population. Tariffs would reduce the competitiveness of 'foreign', that is to say, mainly British, industrial imports, thus giving Irish entrepreneurs an opportunity to supply the home market.

The north, being less populous and more prosperous, had less need of employment than the south, where emigration had been a serious problem since the middle of the preceding century. Moreover, the imposition of tariffs on Irish imports from other countries might provoke retaliation. Since most of the output of northern industries was exported, the effect might prove extremely damaging to the region. In the event, the two parts of the country went their separate ways in 1921. Southern Ireland won its independence. Yet it did not immediately implement the tariff policy its leaders had been advocating. It was force of circumstances, not nationalist ideology, which led to the imposition of tariffs.

THE ERA OF PROTECTION
1932–1960

In the early 1930s the Great Depression led the major trading nations to put up obstacles to the entry of competing imports in an effort to conserve employment at home. Implemented on an international scale, these policies almost certainly deepened and prolonged the recession. However, once under way, small economies had little alternative but to follow the example of the larger countries. In 1932 a change of government brought Eamon de Valera into office and his government, which was more nationalist in sentiment than its predecessor, adopted a programme of tariffs and quotas (or absolute limits) on a wide range of imported goods. Within a few years the republic of Ireland [hereafter referred to as 'Ireland'] had moved from being one of the most 'open' economies in Europe to being one of the most highly protected.

The immediate effect was the establishment of a large number of enterprises, mostly producing consumer goods, to supply the home market. Processed foods, clothing and textiles, household appliances and motor vehicles were some of the

· IRISH LINEN ·

A committee of the Irish House of Commons in 1709 reported that '. . . linen manufacture is now in a declining condition'. In spite of this, and a number of other similarly pessimistic statements about its condition since, the industry has not only persisted, but at times dominated the economy of the North of Ireland. Linen making all through the eighteenth century was very much a domestic industry carried on in farmhouses and cottages all over the north, swelling the trade of several towns (including Belfast) where linen fairs were held, and generating much of the capital on which the industrial base of the region was built. By 1873, some 175,000 acres were devoted to the growing of flax, and the industry employed some 60,000 people. In terms of exports, the peak was reached just before the First World War. After that date competition from abroad, the Depression and after 1945 the introduction of man-made fabrics brought about a contraction of the industry. Of course, some of this competition for linen originated in the traditional flax growing areas of Northern Ireland. By the early 1970s Ryon yarn was being manufactured in Carrickfergus, Terylene in Kilroot, Acrilan in Coleraine and Orlon and Lycra in Maydown, near Londonderry. There was also a boom in the production of textiles made from mixtures of natural and synthetic materials, which resulted in textiles remaining – with the exception of engineering – the most important industry in Northern Ireland.

LEFT *The linen studio at Ulster Weavers, Belfast.*

ABOVE *Cutting out a linen pattern in Dungannon.*

TOP *Irish tweeds and linen are to be found on sale in shops throughout the island.*

ABOVE RIGHT *The traditional blue flower on growing flax, pictured here in a field at Seaforde, County Down, Northern Ireland.*

RIGHT *Colour woven linen on the examination table; the fabric is exported to the United States, Europe and the Far East to be manufactured into male and female clothing.*

most important of the new businesses. Industrial output and employment rose by about 50 per cent between 1926 and 1936. Scarcity of new materials led to a decline in output during World War II, but renewed growth after the war brought industrial output in the mid-1950s to a point about three times higher than the level recorded in 1926. Industrial employment was then about two-and-a-half times as high.

The establishment of a large number of small companies, insulated from foreign competition and confined to supplying the home market, had certain drawbacks. The restricted opportunities for economies of scale, as well as the comparative immunity from competition, meant high production costs. And dependence on the home market meant that industrial expansion could only proceed as fast as the rest of the economy. During the 1950s agriculture, the dominant sector, experienced bad market conditions and the economy as a whole stagnated. Output and employment in industry grew very little throughout most of the 1950s and emigration, then as now the 'bell-weather' of the Irish economy, began to soar.

INDUSTRIAL PERFORMANCE AND FREE TRADE
1960–1970

The poor performance of industry during the 1950s prompted a radical overhaul of policy. That shift in policy is generally credited to Sean Leamass, de Valera's long-time lieutenant, who succeeded him as prime minister in 1957. Leamass set about turning Irish industry outwards to face world markets with the same energy and efficiency as he had cut them off from the outside world 30 years before, when he implemented de Valera's tariff policy. From about 1960 onwards, industrial policy was devoted to encouraging companies to enter foreign markets by means of export grants and tax concessions. Incentives were also provided for foreign companies setting up factories in Ireland.

The Industrial Development Authority was assigned the task of administering the new policy and attracting foreign companies to Ireland. Over the next decade the volume of industrial output nearly doubled, while employment rose by about 25 per cent. The principal growth was in exports, the volume of which quadrupled in this period. Many Irish companies switched their attention to export markets and they profited from the buoyant economic conditions which prevailed in Great Britain and Europe. In addition, the 1960s saw the arrival in Ireland of the first of what was eventually to become a large number of foreign companies. Most of them were set up to

export to Great Britain (to whose markets Ireland had virtually free access in the 1960s) and the continent. The largest proportion were subsidiaries of American companies, which were then crossing the Atlantic in large numbers to capitalize on the boom in European economies. British and German companies also made large contributions and there was a significant representation of French and Dutch firms. Foreign-owned companies mainly engaged in relatively labour-intensive industries like clothing, textiles and light engineering.

The effect of the new employment opportunities created by these industries was quite dramatic, both on the number of workers directly employed in the new factories and also on pubs, hotels, construction companies, and other sectors which attracted the spending-power of the expanding industrial workforce. The centuries-old pattern of emigration came to a halt. Indeed, in part of the 1960s and early 1970s there was net immigration and Ireland, which had been unique in having a declining population, now became noteworthy for one of the fastest-growing populations in Europe!

INDUSTRIAL PERFORMANCE
1970–86

The world-wide recessions in the middle and late years of the 1970s adversely affected Irish export markets and led to a slow-down in the rate of industrial growth. By comparison with the doubling of output during the 1960s, industrial output rose by only about 60 per cent in the 1970s; employment rose by only about 10 per cent. During the 1980s Irish industry has continued to expand at approximately the same rate. However, there have been some marked changes in the nature of this expansion. On the positive side, the 1970s and 1980s have witnessed a boom in the computer industry and the Industrial Development Authority has been able to attract a large number of foreign, especially American, companies in this field to Ireland.

LEFT As head of the Irish Republic, Eamon de Valera travelled to the United States in 1919 to raise money for his infant state. Later De Valera was to be the chief architect of the protectionist policies which dominated Ireland's economic position until the 1960s.

RIGHT The Pfizer corporation, a large American chemical company with a base in Cork.

HARLAND AND WOLFF

The Belfast skyline has long included the giant booms of Harland and Wolff. Shipbuilding itself dates from as early as 1838, and the present site of the great shipyard has been in use since 1853. There was no evidence at this stage that the area would become a centre for shipbuilding, but all this was changed by Edward Harland who bought out the yard for £5,000 in 1858 and soon founded his famous partnership with Gustav W. Wolff, whose uncle had put up the money for Harland. From this moment onwards, the yard grew. In 1861, there were 500 men employed, by 1900 the figure was 9,000. Harland was the technical partner, Wolff was responsible for the orders. The latter was responsible for establishing links with the famous White Star Line. Starting with the *Oceanic* in 1870, the yard built over 50 ships for this line, and the reputation for reliability and quality was now universal. In 1910 the huge Olympic was launched and there then followed the ill-fated Titanic.

The 'Big Yard' was in fact far more than simply a successful local employer. It was the very heart of loyalist Ulster. The shipyard's employees were overwhelmingly Protestant and the benefits of imperial economic membership, meant that the workforce were at the forefront of the struggle against home rule. Since partition in 1921, the shipyards have, however, shown a fairly continual decline. The demand for ships has never been lower and despite attempts to hold onto a portion of the market, it is to Asia that most orders are going. With its probable death in the forseeable future, a major symbol of the differences between north and south will have gone.

LEFT *All the major White Star liners were built at Harland's. The Celtic was launched in 1901.*

ABOVE AND RIGHT *Harland and Wolff shipyards in Belfast; a symbol of industrial, loyalist and imperial Northern Ireland.*

TOP RIGHT *Interiors of many of the liners were as impressive as the exterior. Here is the first class dining room on the Olympic, which was launched from Belfast in 1901.*

R.M.S. Celtic
Length, 697 ft.
Breadth, 75 ft.
Tonnage, 20,904

ABOVE The Titanic was
fitted with watertight doors,
but the collision damage to
the ship was so extensive
that they failed to save her.

TOP In the wake of the Titanic
disaster of 1912, publicity for luxury
liners put great stress on safety. The
Olympic was sent back to Belfast
where her bulkheads were raised and
extra boats taken on board.

ABOVE A Marconigram from one of
the ships that heard the Titanic's
SOS.

LEFT The Titanic leaving Belfast
lough for her trials on April 1912;
she would sink thirteen days later.

78

It has also been successful in attracting 'high-tech' companies in others sectors, such as pharmaceuticals.

In the main their processes are pollution-free, the enterprises offer highly skilled employment, and their advanced technology holds the promise that the companies will be comparatively insulated from competition. Ireland's transport difficulties, as an island off the European mainland, are minimized by the fact that these industries produce high value/low volume items. This characteristic adds to the attraction of these industries for a country with a highly dispersed population. In economic jargon they are 'footloose' and can be spread around the country in a number of different locations. There is no single geographical concentration of 'high-tech' industry in Ireland which would meet the description of a 'silicon valley' as in California or, as in Scotland, a 'silicon glen'. On the negative side, many of the longer-established companies, including some foreign-owned enteprises, have not been able to survive the downturn. Although many thousands of jobs have been created during the 1980s in newly-established companies, there was a net decline in industrial employment of about 16 per cent in the first six years of the decade.

INDUSTRIAL POLICY TODAY

The experience of the 1980s has prompted some adjustments to the policy which emerged in the early 1960s. But in essence the approach is the same. The core of the policy is tax concessions to manufacturing industry combined with grants towards the cost of capital investment. These incentives are available to both foreign and indigenous enterprises provided they can satisfy the Industrial Development Authority that the projects are likely to make a permanent contribution to employment. Probably the most important incentive is the 10 per cent rate of corporation tax on all manufacturing companies. (This compares with the standard rate of corporation tax of 50 per cent.) Investment grants range from about 25 per cent up to as much as 60 per cent of the cost of plant and equipment. Grants for research and development and for training are also available. A number of agencies provide specialized services at zero or subsidised costs. The most important are the Irish Export Board (Coras Trachtala), which provides overseas marketing assistance, the Institute for Industrial Research and Standards, which provides technical services, the Kilkenny Design Workshops, which provide industrial design, and the Industrial Training Authority (AnCo), which provides industrial training. A state-owned credit institution, the Industrial Credit Corporation, provides loan and equity finance for industry on attractive terms.

These aids are made available within the context of a firm commitment to free trade and the free movement of labour and capital. This commitment was initially made in the early 1960s, when Ireland, along with Great Britain, applied for membership of the European Economic Community. When it seemed that membership was indefinitely postponed by French – or more precisely de Gaulle's – objections to British membership, the Irish government negotiated bilateral tariff reductions with Great Britain. When, by 1970, French objections were overcome, and Ireland and Great Britain entered the EEC, there was a further liberalization of trade. Trade now flows freely between Ireland and the other member states, while the controls on Irish trade with non-members are determined by the Community and are the same for each member state. Foreign-exchange controls remain a matter for the individual members, but in Ireland there is no restriction on movements connected with manufacturing operations in or out of the country. Nor is there any restriction on the movement of expatriate employees of foreign companies.

Integration with the European Community and the loss of sovereignty which that entails have given rise to misgivings in certain sections of the Irish public, mainly the left wing of the political spectrum. Those misgivings have been accentuated by the recent recession, which has increased unemployment and revived emigration. A further source of antipathy is the perception that it is farmers who have largely benefited from membership of the Community, while the urban population has had to bear the brunt of unemployment. Thus, although the Irish electorate approved of entry to the EEC in 1972 by a vote of 4:1 on a large turnout, approval of further steps towards integration, expressed in a referendum in 1987, is more muted: the vote was 2:1 in favour, but less than half of the electorate turned out. The result suggests that the average Irish voter feels that on balance membership has helped to improve farm incomes and to secure jobs in industries exporting to EEC member states. But the margin of advantage is seen to have shrunk and enthusiasm for the Community has correspondingly declined.

FOREIGN INVESTMENT

Of the total of about 1,500 foreign owned companies established in Ireland since 1960, about 35% came from the U.S. However, U.S. projects have tended to be much larger than the projects from other countries as witness the fact that U.S. com-

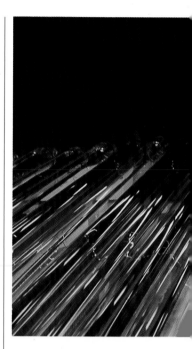

LEFT *Thermomax Ltd, Bangor. The company has won major awards for its evacuated heat pipe solar collectors; a technology for the future which is a far cry from the peat diggers of Connemara.*

BELOW LEFT *The human cost of Ireland's longstanding economic problems: a beggar with a child in the centre of Dublin.*

panies account for over 50% of the total cumulative investment. Most of the larger U.S. companies, especially in the computer, chemicals and health care industries, are represented in Ireland, including IBM, Digital Equipment Corporation (DEC), Wang, Pfizer, Merck, Sharpe & Dohme, Abbott and Eli Lilly. The next most important source of investment is Britain, which supplied about 25% of the total number of foreign owned projects setting up in Ireland. However, British involvement in Irish Industry is probably understated by this figure since many British companies have been in Ireland since before 1960 and several others have invested in Ireland through acquisition rather than through setting up new plants. Among the larger U.K. manufacturing companies in Ireland are ICL, Unilever, Whessoe, Courtaulds, Beecham Group, British Oxygen Corporation, and Racal. Germany is the country with the third largest number of industrial projects in Ireland and accounts for 18% of the total. Important German companies engaged in manufacturing in Ireland include Braun, Krupps, Faber Kastell, Nixdorf, and Siemens. A number of well known Japanese companies have also set up plants in Ireland including Asahi, Brother, NEC, Fuzitsu and Misui Denman. Well known companies of other nationalities now established in Ireland include Ciba-Geigy, Nestlé and Brown Boveri (Switzerland); Douwe Egbert, Philips, and Akzo (Netherlands); ACEC (Belgium); and Hanimax (Australia).

DOMESTIC INDUSTRY

The comparative success of the programme of attracting foreign industry in the 1960s and the 1970s led policy-makers to overlook the performance of Irish-owned industries. Irish-owned companies have been the source of most of the recent job losses (although foreign-owned industry has also shed labour). There are many reasons for the greater vulnerability of Irish companies. Most of them are small by international standards and they are concentrated in sectors like food, building-materials, paper and printing, which have tended to have slow-growing markets. Except for food companies, few of them are major exporters and during the 1970s and 1980s many of the them proved unable to maintain their hold on the home market against competition from imports.

Even so, a number of Irish-owned companies have established a major presence both home and abroad and have achieved comparatively high profiles in American and British markets. Some of them have their origins in the 19th, and even the 18th century. The outstanding example is Arthur Guinness

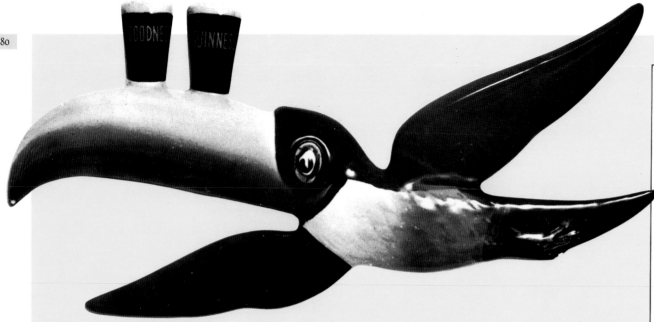

There's nothing like a GUINNESS

ABOVE The advertisements for Guinness are as famous as the drink itself. The toucan has been a regular symbol for the dark beer, introduced in the 1950s.

RIGHT There's also nothing like a good advertising slogan! Guinness have in the past approached some of Ireland's most famous writers – including Brendan Behan, a spectacularly self-destructive drinker himself – to provide advertising copy.

BELOW The changing face of Guinness labels, left to right, from 1890 to 1983.

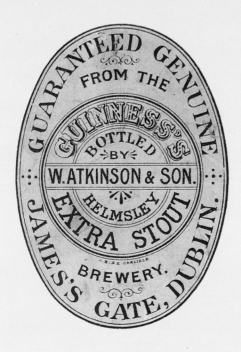

· GUINNESS ·

Ireland is one of the biggest exporters of beer in Europe. Almost all of it is Guinness, a stout; a great deal of it is exported to Britain (despite the existence of a very large Guinness brewery in London).

The rumour has persisted for many years that Guinness tastes better in Ireland; often the difference is fancifully attributed to the water of Dublin's River Liffey. In fact, a more likely explanation is simply that Irish Guinness in both draught and bottled form is unpasteurized. The brewery was founded in 1759. By 1890 it was the biggest in the world. The Anglo-Irish Guinness family have maintained a close control over, and interest in, the company since its inception until very recently.

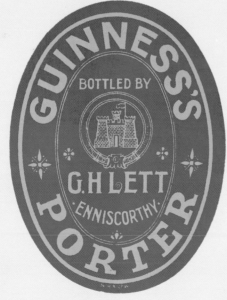

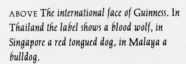

ABOVE *Guinness became so popular that it was bottled and sold under licence by rival brewers.*

ABOVE *The international face of Guinness. In Thailand the label shows a blood wolf, in Singapore a red tongued dog, in Malaya a bulldog.*

TOP *Another Guinness advertising aphorism, this time in the native Irish.*

ABOVE *Traditional wooden casks; still the best way to keep Guinness, but impractical for such huge exports.*

Son & Co, the brewing company which was founded in the 19th century and which through most of its existence was one of the largest enterprises in the country. The company remained under the effective control of the Guinness family until quite recently. As in the manner of British industrialists (Ireland was under British rule during most of the company's existence), members of the family entered the British aristocracy. But the family's links with Ireland, like the company's, have remained strong and have been expressed down the years in support for various charitable foundations in Ireland. Guinness, as the company is now simply called, moved its headquarters to London in the 1930s. In recent years it has grown rapidly, through acquisitions, and has become a multinational corporation.

Other companies with a long history in the country include John Jameson & Son, John Power & Son and the Cork Distilleries Company. These enterprises remained family companies until the mid-1960s, when they merged to form the Irish Distillers Group. The merger came not a moment too soon for the good of the Irish distilling industry. Until the early part of this century, Irish whiskey dominated the world market, but the independent-mindedness of the Irish family companies contributed to a comparative failure of the industry to develop. By contrast, Scotch Whisky producers, partly by combining into a small number of large companies, gradually displaced the Irish from their premier position in the market. However, it may be that the fortunes of the Irish spirit are beginning to revive: certainly recent years have witnessed a steady expansion in the home and export sales of the Irish Distillers Group.

The largest Irish-owned manufacturing company is the Jefferson Smurfit Group, a paper and packaging manufacturer. It was established in the 1930s, during the era of protection, by Jefferson Smurfit, an English emigrant and a tailor by profession. In the mid-1960s the company, still under his control, went public. In the 1970s the Jefferson Smurfit Group began a programme of international expansion. A series of well-timed acquisitions in Great Britain and the United States has made the company one of the largest paper and packaging manufacturers in the world. International sales exceed £1 billion. Despite its greatly expanded size and geographical diversification, the company is still under the control of the Smurfit family and the international headquarters remain in Dublin.

The European Community's common agricultural policy has led to growth in milk production and to improved markets for meat, and since 1972 the Irish dairy industry, dominated by farmer-owned cooperatives, has expanded rapidly. Leading Irish

dairy cooperatives include Kerry, Avonmore, Waterford and Golden Vale, with sales ranging from £150 million to £250 million a year. Initially involved only in the processing of milk, these companies have diversified into other food products and are increasingly involved in high value-added branded products.

One of the best-known products is 'Kerrygold', a brand of butter marketed by the Irish Dairy Board. The marketing of this product was the first success story of the Irish food-processing industry. The architect of the success was Tony O'Reilly, a charismatic figure who first achieved international fame for his exploits on the rugby field. Sadly for Ireland, 'Kerrygold' was O'Reilly's last major contribution to Irish food exports. Shortly after leaving the Irish Dairy Board he moved to the Heinz Corporation in Philadelphia, where he is now chairman and chief executive. Under his management, this multinational food company has had a remarkable record of consistent growth.

The contribution of Irish-owned companies to the domestic economy has not been commensurate with their success as individual commercial organizations. The fastest-growing owe most of their success to investment overseas; their Irish operations have tended to be static. It is true that the food industries have placed most of their investments at home near their supplies of raw materials. But the bulk of their output still comprises commodity products such as milk powder, carcass meat and butter, which require comparatively little processing and so generate few jobs. There are, however, companies which have managed to combine growth with heavy investment in Ireland. The most widely known is the Waterford Glass Group. This company was formed in 1951 by Joe McGrath, whose most noteworthy venture until then – the Irish Hospitals Sweepstakes – was almost as well known to an earlier generation of Americans as Waterford Glass is to the present generation. Joe McGrath's objective was to revive the 19th-century tradition of Irish glass craftsmanship and the company has proved an outstanding success. It represents an ideal model for Irish industrialization. Its output comprises high-value products, its processes are labour-intensive, its raw materials are found at home and its markets are mainly abroad. In recent years the company has grown through acquisitions and the influence of the McGrath family in its affairs has faded. (The family's earlier enterprise, the Hospital Sweepstakes, has also recently been folded up.) Many attempts have been made to emulate the features of the Waterford company, in glass and other industries, and some have enjoyed a measure of success. But none has yet attained Waterford Glass's size or profitability.

· WHISKEY ·

Monks from the Continent probably brought the art of distilling to Ireland some time during the fifth and sixth centuries, but it was the native Irish who developed and refined the specialized art of distilling whiskey; they kept the good news to themselves until the invasion of the English King Henry II in the twelfth century, whose troops quickly developed a taste for *uisce beatha*. In 1608, Sir Thomas Phillips, the deputy of King James I in Ulster, granted the first official licence to distill – to himself – and Old Bushmills, indisputably the oldest licensed distillery in the world, began production. The exceptionally smooth and light taste of Irish whiskey is the result of its unique triple distillation. In addition, at the start of the malting process the Irish halt the germination of the barley by heating it with a coal fire in a closed oven, unlike the Scots, who dry the grain in an open kiln over a smoky peat fire. The barley thus never acquires the peat reek that characterizes scotch. Someone complained to President Lincoln about General Ulysses S Grant's overfondness for Irish whiskey. Lincoln replied: 'Find out his brand and give it to the other generals.'

BELOW There were once hundreds of distilleries in Ireland, north and south, but now all whiskey is produced either at Midleton – albeit retaining the old distilling, blending and maturing methods and thus preserving the unique flavours and characteristics of each label – or at Bushmills.

ABOVE The customs and excise man at Midleton; by the late eighteenth century, there were about 2,000 whiskey stills in Ireland. Many of these were extremely small and therefore, according to an official report, 'well placed to avoid the revenue'. The distillers of poteen, a fiery, occasionally dangerous, unaged spirit, are of course still doing just that, all over Ireland.

LEFT The huge copper pot stills at the Midleton distillery complex, County Cork; opened in 1975, the complex was the outcome of a much-needed rationalization of the whiskey industry, after the four great distillers – John Powers and Sons, Tullamore Dew, John Jameson and Sons, and Cork Distilleries – (and later Old Bushmills), came together as the Irish Distillers Group to take up the challenge thrown down by the Scots.

86

STATE INDUSTRY

In addition to stimulating both private domestic and foreign companies to invest in Ireland, the government also plays a direct role in commercial activity through a number of state companies. As in most European countries, the aggregate size of the state sector is large. In all there are about two dozen state companies in transport, communications, energy, manufacturing and finance. In total they employ about 78,000 persons, have a turnover of £4 billion and net assets of £7 billion, compared with a turnover of £13 billion and employment of 195,000 persons in the private industrial sector. The largest state company in terms of employment is Telecom Eireann, the national telephone company; the largest in terms of turnover and assets employed is the Electricity Supply Board.

The establishment of state companies was not the result of a conscious programme of nationalization. The companies were started or acquired because private companies had tried and failed to provide vital products or services, or because the private sector had not tried at all. Examples of companies which had failed include the Irish Sugar Company, restarted in state hands in the 1930s, the Irish Life Assurance, formed in the 1930s from a number of failed private insurance companies, and Coras Iompair Eireann (the national transport company), formed in the 1940s from the bankrupt railways and other ground transport companies. Companies which were started by the state include the national airline, Aer Lingus, the Electricity Supply Board, and the organization which eventually became Telecom Eireann, the national telecommunications company.

In state hands, these companies have enjoyed varying fortunes. Until recently their financial performance appeared reasonably impressive. But in many cases it was greatly assisted by free capital from the government and privileges in the form of monopoly positions, tariffs against competing imports and other controls on competition. The removal of these privileges, and the general growth in competition in the energy, transport, finance and manufacturing sectors, have revealed shortcomings. Some enterprises have managed to surmount these challenges. A notable example is Irish Life. Concentrating almost exclusively on life assurance in an openly competitive market, it has accumulated assets of £2.5 billion and established a major presence in the British market. Another state company which is deemed to have performed well is Aer Lingus, which has supplemented slender profits from its air transport operations by a programme of diversification into foreign

Cork International Airport. The modern face of Irish enterprise, the interlinking of the country with the rest of Europe. The airport was opened in 1961, and now handles over 450,000 passengers a year. Interestingly, as a pointer to the level of Irish integration with the rest of the world, there are no transatlantic flights.

88

RIGHT *Temtech Ltd, Bangor: the company manufactures cardiac defibrillators which are sold worldwide.*

FAR RIGHT *The Chemical Vapour deposition plant at the Bio-Engineering centre, University of Ulster.*

BELOW *Ryanair at Dublin Airport, one of the homegrown Irish economic success stories; Ryanair has been succeeding in the highly competitive market of air traffic.*

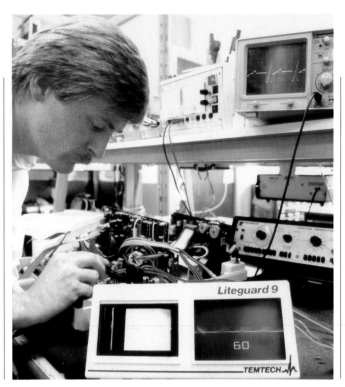

markets for ancillary services. The company now runs a string of operations from hotels in Boston to hospitals in Baghdad. Another state company which has managed to make its mark overseas is the Electricity Supply Board, which has developed a major business in providing consultancy and project management services to underdeveloped countries.

NATURAL RESOURCES

Until about 30 years ago the conventional wisdom in Ireland was that the country had no mineral or energy resources. The only significant indigenous energy source was peat, exploited on a systematic basis by Bord na Mona (the Peat Board) since the 1940s. There was also an extractive industry engaged in the quarrying of stone, slate and gravel for the building industry. In total, however, these extractive activities were small, accounting for less than five per cent of total industrial employment during the 1950s and making virtually no contribution to exports. The perception of the country as poor in mineral and energy resources changed in the 1960s after the discovery of lead-zinc ore in County Galway and the introduction of tax concessions for the mining industry. These developments prompted an upsurge in exploratory activity – mainly by North American companies – and in the following years there were a number of finds of lead, zinc, copper and silver in various parts of the country. This phase of the development of the Irish mining industry culminated in a lead and zinc find in County Meath by Tara Mines Exploration and Development. This proved to be the biggest lead-zinc ore deposit in Europe and one of the biggest in the world. As a result of these discoveries the output of the extractive industries in Ireland increased by 230 per cent during the 1960s.

Following the discovery of the Navan ore body there was a decline in exploratory efforts, partly because of the adverse economic climate of the late 1970s. At the same time, output of some of the older mines were beginning to wind down. Over the decade, therefore, output of the extractive industries rose by only 33 per cent. Popular concern about the environment may also have hindered development. It led, for instance, to the cancellation of a potential open-cast mining operation in the Irish midlands. On the whole, however, there are still too few operations to give rise to significant concern for the environment. A more material factor in halting expansion is that since 1980 three of the larger mines have been exhausted. Extraction of gypsum, slate and other building materials has also been adversely affected by the recession. Output of the extrac-

tive industries fell by almost one-third in the first half of the 1980s. But mineral exploration and development is a cyclical business and in the mid-1980s there has been a revival of efforts by Irish exploration companies. There seems to be a good chance that a new phase of development of the mining industry is about to begin.

Exploration both on and off shore for hydrocarbon resources, led to the discovery by the Marathon company of an offshore gas field near Kinsale, in County Cork, in 1971. This field went into production in 1978 at an average daily rate of 162.5 million cubic feet – enough to meet about 20 per cent of the country's annual energy needs. This find, and the prevalence of high oil prices during most of the 1970s, led to considerable exploration in Irish waters. So far it has not yielded fruit. The drilling of 95 exploration wells (to the end of 1986) has yielded no commercially viable finds. And the number of wells drilled has tended to fall off in recent years. On the other hand, from a number of wells have flowed small quantities of oil, enough to encourage the exploration companies to continue their efforts, albeit at a lower level than in the 1970s.

INDUSTRY IN NORTHERN IRELAND

While the southern Irish state adopted a policy of protection in the 1930s, industry in northern Ireland remained fully exposed to competition with the rest of Great Britain. By the 1930s the two staple industries of the north, linen and shipbuilding, were in deep depression. The war years witnessed a recovery in the fortunes of shipbuilding, but by the end of the 1950s the long-term decline in both industries was well underway. Together they employed 80,000 workers in 1950; today there are fewer than 6,000 people employed in the shipyards and the linen industry is under pressure. The response of the authorities to the adverse trends of the 1950s was similar to that in the south. Government agencies were established and financial incentives extended to attract investment from outside the province. As in the south, these measures enjoyed a degree of success. In particular a number of large manufacturing subsidiaries of British companies set up throughout Northern Ireland. However, the 1970s saw a reversal. Competition from third-world producers of textiles, world-wide recession and the 'Troubles' led to the withdrawal of many multinationals.

Current policy is to focus on encouraging investment in small, locally-owned enterprises, which are considered to have a better chance of long-term success than some of the larger foreign-owned companies. In addition, orders from the British

Beamish and Murphy are brewers of stout, rivals to Guinness, but producing on a much smaller scale. Lett's was the last small independent brewery, which ceased production in 1956. The firm now licenses its popular ruby ale to the Pelforth brewery.

OPPOSITE *The Waterford Crystal factory; the company has long been one of the flagships of Irish enterprise and skill.*

LEFT *The harbour development at Cork. An example of the many attempts to modernize declining areas through a partnership of public and private investment.*

government have helped keep Harland & Wolff shipbuilders in business. The Shorts aircraft company is also enjoying considerable success in the production of light aircraft, with subcontracts from larger aircraft companies in the United States and Great Britain.

The last 60 years have seen a radical transformation in the structure of Irish industry. In 1922 the northern Irish economy was an industrialized one, with about 200,000 people – or 40 per cent of the workforce – engaged in industry. In the south industry employed about 100,000 people about 10 per cent of the workforce. Now the northern Irish economy is in the process of deindustrialization – an experience it is sharing with many of the other long-industrialized parts of Europe and North America. Industrial employment today is half what it was 60 years ago. In the south, by contrast, industrial employment has about doubled – with about 25 per cent of the work force – and industry is now equally important in both areas. In its even spread the pattern of industrializaton in the island has reverted to what it was in the 19th century, before Belfast's supremacy in shipbuilding and linen manufacture made itself felt. What has not changed in the last hundred years – nor indeed in the last two hundred years – is Irish industry's heavy dependence on exports for survival. Nor have the destinations of Irish exports changed very much. Great Britain, North America and Europe remain the dominant trading partners.

The significant change in both parts of the country has been in the pattern ownership of industry. Until 1945 the bulk of industry was owned by Irish residents. Foreign investment in both parts of the country in the last two decades and the decline in traditional industries have changed the picture. The new industries bring employment, new technology and access to foreign markets; but, as experience in Ireland and elsewhere has shown, the commitment of foreign-owned companies to a host economy is far less than to the economy of their domicile. The challenge facing both parts of Ireland is therefore to find policies which will revive the spirit of local enterprise, the enterprise which, less than 100 years ago, made Ireland one of the leading industrial economies of the day.

Some examples of the magnificent level of craftsmanship attained at the Waterford glass factory. Joe McGrath's dream of the revival of the nineteenth century tradition of Irish glass workmanship has been fully realized. The sign (right) indicates the number of foreign visitors – and potential customers – who are attracted to the factory.

• PEAT •

Peat bogs cover about six per cent of Ireland's surface. They are a legacy of colder climatic conditions than prevail today. The water-logged soil and the cold created an environment unfavourable to bacterial decay, so that vegetation accumulating year after year was not incorporated into the soil. This accumulation of debris has provided cheap fuel in the form of turf for the great mass of the Irish population. The old method of preparing it was to dig it out in slabs three or four feet long with specially shaped spades called 'slanes'. The slabs were then stacked to dry, which took about six weeks. Peat burns with a red, smoky flame and a strong smell.

Peat landscapes of the west; FAR LEFT, *the Ring of Kerry,* LEFT AND ABOVE LEFT, *County Donegal,* AND ABOVE, *just a few miles from Galway. Some peat is now machine-dug: digging by hand is cold, backbreaking work. Peat as a fuel in Ireland is no quaint anachronism: the boilerhouses of Shannon airport are run on it.*

OPPOSITE, LEFT *Not so much as a twig in sight and no coal for the mission settlement on Achill Island, established in 1834 by the Reverend Edward Nangle; in landscapes such as this, peat played a vital role in the economic structure of society.*

96

ABOVE LEFT AND LEFT *Killybegs,*
County Donegal; the importance of the
fishing industry lies in its effect on local
communities. The industry is not on the
same commercial scale as in, say, Iceland.

ABOVE *Circuit boards are exported*
worldwide from Craigavon; the
industries of the north and south depend
equally heavily on export for survival.

IRISH LITERATURE
IN THE
TWENTIETH CENTURY

Yeats's tower, Thorballylee; a home of the
Anglo-Irishman who assumed the leadership
of the Irish literary revival at the end of the
19th century. He was to become one of the
first senators of the Irish Free State and won
the Nobel prize for Literature in 1923.

The difficulty which confronts anyone undertaking a survey of Irish writing in English in this century is an embarrassment of riches. The temptation is simply, like W B Yeats, to 'murmur name upon name'. Certainly there are any number of names to murmur. There are poets: Yeats himself, whose genius overshadows so many other fine writers in the generation immediately after him – Austin Clarke, Patrick Kavanagh, Louis MacNiece – and from whose influence many contemporary poets are still trying to free themselves – Seamus Heaney, Thomas Kinsella, John Montague, Derek Mahon, Tom Paulin, Eavan Boland and Paul Muldoon. Then there is the Irish impact on the theatre through the work of Oscar Wilde, G B Shaw, J M Synge, Sean O'Casey, Lady Gregory, Brendan Behan, Samuel Beckett and Brian Friel. And finally there are the novelists and short-story writers by whose work our idea of the novel and

BELOW *The Parnell monument, O'Connell Street, Dublin; Irish writing has always been involved in the national struggle. Parnell's fall in 1890, after proof of his adultery with the wife of Captain William O'Shea, coincided with the beginning of the great cultural advances of that decade. There is a profound ambiguity in the reactions of writers like Yeats to famous Irish political figures, depicting them both as heroes and monsters; as part of what he called 'all that delirium of the brave'.*

OPPOSITE *Trinity College, Dublin; the symbol of Anglo-Irish society, and of an attitude best summed up by Yeats, who considered that Protestant Ireland had 'created most of the modern literature of the country'.*

the short story has been radically altered: James Joyce, George Moore, Frank O'Connor, Sean O'Faolain, Liam O'Flaherty, Flann O'Brien, Francis Stuart, Elizabeth Bowen, Mary Lavin and, among contemporary writers, Brian Moore, Aidan Higgins, John Banville, Julia O'Faolain and John McGahern.

To add to the difficulty, many of these writers do not fit a single category. Beckett is perhaps best known as a playwright, but he is also a major novelist. O'Casey's reputation rests on his plays, but his autobiography is a masterpiece. And although the word 'Irish' applies to all of these writers, it fails to convey the range and diversity of their backgrounds: there are southern and northern writers, Roman Catholic, Protestant, mystic and atheist writers, rural and urban writers.

The impact of this wealth of names is twofold: one is awestruck at the richness of Ireland's literary culture and at the same time puzzled as to how such a small island could have produced it. There are some standard explanations for this phenomenon. According to some people, Ireland hurts its writers into poetry; that is to say, the wealth of Irish literature is somehow related to the turbulence of Irish history. Others consider the reason to be an Irish love of and zest for language. Yet others argue that Irish literature has its roots in the rich imagination of the Irish people. None of these answers is satisfactory, however, because none of them explain the rapid development of Irish literature in English in the 20th century. Surely Irish history was turbulent before the beginning of this century and surely the Irish loved language before this century and surely the Irish imagination was rich before this century? Perhaps, instead of considering why Ireland has produced the writing it has, it is better to ask why it is that this writing has been so widely acclaimed? Irish writing is loved throughout the world. Go to Japan and you will find enthusiastic students of Yeats poetry; go to France and Joyce and Beckett are acknowledged as masters; in America it is possible to study the full range of Irish writing at numerous colleges. Why are the literary products of this small, green corner of the universe so widely regarded? It is certainly not because Irish writers have pandered to outside tastes and attitudes.

The best Irish writers, like Joyce, Yeats or Synge, are obsessive about the nature of life in Ireland. Their work demands from their readers a curiosity about Irish life. Joyce assumes that his readers will be interested in what it is to grow up as a Catholic in Dublin; Yeats' poetry confronts the problems of establishing a national culture for Ireland; O'Casey plays demand from the audience an interest in the plight of the Dublin

TO CHARLES STEWART PARNELL

NO MAN HAS A RIGHT TO FIX THE BOUNDARY TO THE MARCH OF A NATION NO MAN HAS A RIGHT TO SAY TO HIS COUNTRY THUS FAR SHALT THOU GO AND NO FURTHER WE HAVE NEVER ATTEMPTED TO FIX THE NE PLUS ULTRA TO THE PROGRESS OF IRELAND'S NATIONHOOD AND WE NEVER SHALL

working class in the wake of the Easter Rising of 1916. Irish writing is often inward-looking and it is a point of principle with many Irish writers that it should be. Two very different writers, the cosmopolitan novelist, George Moore, and the 'peasant' poet, Patrick Kavanagh, stressed this in their works. For Moore it was axiomatic that art had to be parochial before it could be cosmopolitan; it had to concentrate on its roots, on those things from which it grew, before it would be worthy of wider attention. Kavanagh, too, believed that the only worthwhile art was that which concentrated on its own issues; if it did so, then it would be respected for its integrity. The stage-Irishman, that caricature of the Irishman as buffoon, stands as a warning of what happens when the writer betrays his roots in order to gain a wider audience. Yet Irish writing must also have a relevance for that wider audience if it is to succeed, and in these areas in particular Irish writing has managed to concern itself with the matter of Ireland while at the same time having something to say to the world: about language, politics, and community.

LANGUAGE

All writers must pay attention to their language, must strive to make it do exactly what they want. For the Irish writer who uses English this requirement is complicated by the fact of dealing with a 'foreign' language. Even if a writer has been brought up as an English speaker, there is a sense, as Yeats put it, that English is a mother tongue rather than a native language. The Irish writer has to express himself in a language which has been formed by another culture and a different history. The most famous encounter between an Irish writer and the English language occurs in Joyce's autobiographical novel, A *portrait of the Artist as a Young Man*, in which the hero, Stephen Dedalus, has a discussion with an English priest leading to these thoughts:

The language in which we are speaking is his before it is mine. How different are the words home, Christ, ale, master *on his lips and on mine! His language, so familiar and so foreign, will always be for me an acquired speech. I have not made or accepted its words.*

The whole of Joyce's career, from the 'scrupulous meanness' of his early short stories in *Dubliners* to the extravagant dream-language of *Finnegans Wake*, can be seen as, among other things, a struggle to take the English language and twist and mould it into his own instrument. The multiple puns and grammatical

· WILLIAM BUTLER YEATS ·

Yeats began his literary work translating Gaelic tales and compilations of Irish folklore. His early original verse was strongly influenced by Irish myth. Later poems explored Irish politics and his (unrequited) love for Maud Gonne, the Irish actress and patriot, who was a founder of Sinn Fein. The breadth of association of his writing (which included verse plays and folk stories as well as poetry), is daunting, from Irish legend to eastern philosophy, mysticism and magic. A late poem, however (*The Circus Animals' Desertion*) expresses a belief in the inevitable return for the poet in search of inspiration to the place

where all things start
In the foul rag and bone shop of the heart.

ABOVE *Ben Bulben, north Sligo; famed in legend as the place where Diarmuid, the hero of the epic the Pursuit of Diarmuid and Grainne was killed while taking part in a boar hunt. Much of Yeats's poetry is steeped in such Irish folklore and imagery, and legendary figures are introduced into poems about modern political figures:*

When Pearse summoned
Cuchulain to his side,
Who stalked through the Post Office?
In these lines from The Statues Pearse is Patrick Henry Pearse, the nationalist leader and writer executed after the Easter uprising of 1916 (the Dublin post office was destroyed in the rebellion); Cuchulain is the legendary Irish warrior.

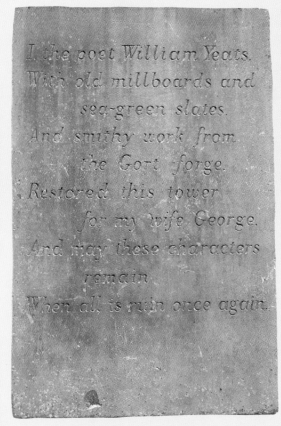

I, the poet William Yeats,
With old millboards and
sea-green slates,
And smithy work from
the Gort forge,
Restored this tower
for my wife George.
And may these characters
remain
When all is ruin once again.

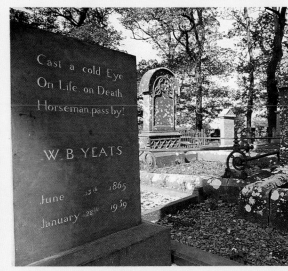

Cast a cold Eye
On Life, on Death.
Horseman pass by!

W. B YEATS

June   13th 1865
January 28th 1939

OPPOSITE, FAR LEFT
The Isle of Innisfree,
Yeats's inspiration for
the lyrical poem
(quoted on page 48),
expressing the desire
for solitude and a
return to the values of
an ancient, Celtic
Ireland.

FAR LEFT AND
BELOW LEFT
*Yeats's grave at
Drumcliff, County
Sligo; the epitaph he
wrote himself.*

LEFT *Yeats's
own inscription set
into the tower at
Thorballylee; Yeats
bought the tower and
lived and worked in it
in the summer months
of the 1920s.*

104

innovations of *Finnegans Wake* are an extreme form of such manipulation. But Joyce was not alone among Irish writers in feeling the need to make English fit his purposes. Nearly every major Irish writer set out to take English and, in Seamus Heaney's phrase, 'make it eat stuff it had never eaten before'. The plays of Synge record the encounter between Irish thought and English expression, producing a language which Synge described as being 'as fully flavoured as a nut or apple'. The poetry of Yeats moves from the highly poetical style of such early 'Celtic Twilight' poems as 'He wishes for the Cloths of Heaven' and 'The Secret Rose' to the language 'cold and passionate as the dawn' of 'The Fisherman'. Flann O'Brien's elaborate puns, for instance in his most famous novel, *At Swim-Two-Birds*, echo the layers of reality of which his Ireland is composed.

At the other extreme from O'Brien there are writers such as Sean O'Faolain and John McGahern, whose work is characterised by a flat, exact style, a reaction to linguistic over-abundance which was possible for them because Joyce and others had already proved that the Irish writer was capable of dominating the English language. The struggle with language, however, never ends. Each Irish writer has, it seems, still to come to terms with English and form it for his own use. Kavanagh's desire to play 'a tune on a flat string' was a desire to express

Ask an Englishman where this image of clipped lawn and students' bicycles comes from, and he will probably answer Oxford or Cambridge; which for many years was quite the intention. Until as late as 1970 it was a sin for any Roman Catholic to study here, at Trinity College. Such a situation was bound to influence the writing of the college's graduates in later years.

heightened emotions in an everyday language. In 'Station Island' Seamus Heaney speaks with the ghosts of various past writers, Joyce and Kavanagh included, whose lesson for him is that the Irish have established a right to the English language, that they have taken something imposed upon them and made it their own. This sense of proprietorship has led to some interesting developments. The poet, Tom Paulin, in his most recent collection of poems, *Liberty Tree*, has begun to explore the idiosyncrasies of norther Irish English with both intelligence and wit. His contemporary, John Morrow, has also exploited the verbal richness of the Belfast dialect in his short stories and novels. The difficulty is that a non-Irish, even a non-Belfast, audience may find certain words incomprehensible – 'oxter', 'dander', 'gaunch' to give a few examples – words which they will not find in the standard dictionaries. But both Paulin and Morrow are upholding a tradition and that tradition of an uncompromising approach to language helps to explain the reputation enjoyed by Irish writing in English.

That uncompromising use of language bespeaks an integrity which has to be admired even if the language itself is at times difficult to understand; and at the same time it reflects the experience of vast numbers of people. Millions of people speak a language which is not native to them. Successive waves of emigrants to the United States have to leave behind their own language and turn to English; and English, while it is the national language of North America, is not native to it, but has had to be remoulded into American English to fit the American experience. Nor is this phenomenon confined to English. Languages such as Spanish and French have spread far beyond their countries of origin to become the daily language of millions. The experience of the Irish writer is therfore both relevant and instructive for people of many cultures.

POLITICS

When an Irish writer uses language there will always be a political significance to his work. Frank O'Connor said that he knew of 'no other literature so closely linked to the immediate reality of politics'. In the first quarter of the century the politics of Irish writing had overridingly to do with the formation of a new Ireland independent of Great Britain. Sean O'Faolain has pointed out that literature did not just record the revolutionary transformation of Ireland; it was a part of that transformation, 'a whole people giving tongue, and by that self-articulation approaching nearer than ever before to intellectual and imaginative freedom'. The Rising of 1916 was not a singular

· GAELIC ·

Gaelic is part of a family of Celtic languages that includes the Gaulish languages which died out in the early Christian period, the Britannic forms from which came Welsh, Cornish and Breton; and the Goidelic from which Irish, Scottish Gaelic and Manx developed. With the coming of Christianity to Ireland a written script developed and the great sagas, folktales, genealogies and laws were recorded. These make it one of the oldest literatures in Europe. Added to the secular material was a growing body of devotional works; in particular, prayers, lives of the Saints and elegies. In 597 Dallan Forgaill composed an elegy to St Colum Cille, which is the oldest surviving composition that can be dated with assurance.

Between the period 900 and 1200 Old Irish, which was difficult and confined to the scholarly class, gave way to the less rigid forms of Middle Irish. The vernacular speech of the people increasingly became part of the written tradition. In spite of the fact that the country had no political unity, consisting of hundreds of minor kingdoms, no written dialects developed. The language of the ordinary people may well have contained important regional variations but the written language was unified.

Seačt mná if feaff caimg ale.   le macfb Mileaò fle
Téa, Fial, Fáf feifoe oe.   liobfa, Oòba, Scoc, Sgéine
Téa bean Eifiomoin na neač.   Fial fóf fa bean oo lfgòioč
Fáf beán Uim mic Uige iaf fin.   if Sgéine blf aimifgin
liobfa bean Fuaio cóin ablaò.   Scoca ancóncuma if Oòba
ag fin na mná nač af mlf.   caimg le macfb Miliob.

Seven ladies of the chiefeft quality
Followed the fortunes of the ftout Milefians:
When they refolved to conquer or to die.
Tea, the virtuous queen of *Heremon*;
Fial the confort of the brave *Lughaidh*;
Fais was a princefs of diftinguifhed beauty,
And the beloved wife of *Un*; and *Sceine*
Was wedded to *Amergin*'s princely bed;
Liobhradh was the royal pride of *Fuaid*:
Scota, the relict of the great *Milefius*,
And *Oghbha*, ftrictly chafte in widowhood.

The Early Modern period saw the rise of a Bardic school of writing which culminated in a great flowering of poetry and prose in the seventeenth century – the century which saw the final collapse of Gaelic culture during the English reconquest of Ireland. It was partly a realization by the poets that as the armies criss-crossed Ireland something of that old world had to be salvaged for the future. As Geoffrey Keating prefaced his task of compiling his History of Ireland, it was not fitting that 'so honourable a land as Eire and kindreds so noble as those who had inhabited it, should pass away without mention or report of them'. What remained of Irish learning was passed on by exiles, cut off from the roots of the language among the common people, or in the hedge-schools of the poor who had neither access to printing presses or the means of supporting the poets or scholars of the language. The new élite were mainly English speaking and few had either sufficient knowledge or

interest to cultivate the ancient language. In that period, between the decline of aristocratic patronage for poetry and the rise of a literate middle class for commercial publishers, the continuity of Gaelic literature was lost.

Ireland from the early nineteenth century increasingly developed as an English speaking society; and not all the efforts of various language revival groups has managed to halt, let alone reverse the trend. Even the Irish *Gaeltacht*, where the people use Irish as their daily vernacular, has diminished greatly. In the post-Famine period well over a million still spoke the language; at the time of Irish Independence in 1921, this figure had fallen to about a quarter of a million. By the Second World War the number of native speakers had fallen to about one hundred thousand and today it is probably less than half that number. Of course there has been a great rise in the numbers who have a passing knowledge of Gaelic since it is the official language of the state and is a compulsory subject in schools, but this has done little to make it the spoken language of the home.

· JAMES JOYCE ·

James Joyce (1882–1941) was the first of ten children born to Mary and John Joyce, tax-collector, drinker, ne'er-do-well and general *bon vivant*, in County Dublin. The young Joyce was educated at Clongowes Wood College, and later at Belvedere, a Jesuit secondary school. After graduating from University College, Dublin, he emigrated to Paris to study medicine while supporting himself by writing and reviewing books for Dublin and London literary magazines. Prompted by his mother's failing health, he returned to Dublin. During this short stay, lodging in the Martello tower with Oliver St John Gogarty, he completed his first collection of short stories, *Dubliners*, but

arguments with the publisher kept it out of print for a further ten years. He met his future wife, Nora Barnacle, in the spring of 1904 and at the end of the year they both departed for the Continent, living in Paris, Trieste and Zurich, where Joyce died in 1941.

While living in Paris, Joyce began his great re-creation of the Dublin of his youth in such works as *Portrait of the Artist as a Young Man* (1916) and *Ulysses* (1922), which were to establish his reputation as one of the foremost writers of the modern period. *Ulysses* was distinctive for its novel literary devices – the 'stream of consciousness' being the most famous – its varied levels of meaning, its verisimilitude of

language, its literary allusions and its attempt to shape the affairs of a group of Dubliners into a structure of significance by the use of classical myth. Its frank discussion of love and sexual desire made the work

one of the most controversial and sought after publications of the period. It was banned, burned, seized by customs, argued about by lawyers, and made the subject of sermons for nearly four decades after its publication. And it was not until the 1960s that it became available for wider public discussion and acknowledgement.

His last great work *Finnegans Wake* was even more problematic. It presented a pot-pourri of literary allusions, puzzles, anecdotes, folklore, linguistic cross-references and puns in a dozen European languages – a great overloading of language and meaning which in its entirety almost defies understanding, but which, in small fragments, can be fascinating and beautiful to the ear. The completed work appeared in 1939, two years before his death.

phenomenon, but the culmination of a process which had been going on in the cultural as much as the overtly political sphere. To read Yeats or Moore or Joyce or Synge is to witness the shaping of a nation; it is to read a literature in which Ireland was coming into being.

This is not to say that Irish writing was at the service of narrowly nationalistic factions. There is a long tradition in Irish writing of criticism of political events. Joyce's story, 'Ivy Day in the Committee Room', like Yeats' 'September 1913', is an expression of indignation at the hypocrisy and petty-mindedness of Irish politicians. The novels of Patrick MacGill and the plays of Sean O'Casey serve as reminders that the national issue was not the political issue of the time; the new Ireland would have to serve its working classes better than the old English-ruled Ireland had done before it could lay claim to their allegiance. The early stories of both Frank O'Connor (*Guest of the Nation*) and Sean O'Faolain (*Midsummer Night Madness*) convey the exhilaration of being young and fighting for one's country, mixed with despair at the futility of civil war.

When the Civil War ended and memories of war faded the political involvement of the writers did not fade away. Instead of striving to form a national culture, writers turned their attention to the condition of the society they had helped to bring about. Much of this social criticism, in the works of O'Faolain, O'Connor and Brinsley MacNamara, was directed at the current state of affairs. A large amount of it, however, was oriented towards the past or rather towards the ways in which the new Ireland was dealing with, and often betraying, its past. Mervyn Wall's *Leaves for the Burning*, the satirical poetry of Austin Clarke and Denis Johnston's play, *The Old Lady Says 'No'*, are very different works which have in common a concern that Ireland should not forget certain aspects of its history, whether by discarding certain traditions or by mythologizing certain events, a different kind of disremembering.

The political function of literature in Ireland has long been to act as a reminder of aspects of Irish life which are in danger of being ignored. Irish literature has striven to encompass all aspects of the nation's experience, especially those which do

• SEAMUS HEANEY •

Heaney (b. 1939) is regarded as one of the most important Irish poets writing today. He was born in County Derry in 1939 and attended St Columb's College and later Queen's University Belfast, where he earned a first class honours degree in English. He became a lecturer at St Joseph's College of Education, and later he returned to Queens. In the 1970s he settled in Dublin, and has since lectured on English literature.

His first book, *Death of a Naturalist* (1966), brought him widespread acclaim as a poet of the northern Irish landscape. It established him as a writer about country details, insignificant in themselves, but which underlie so much of the vocabulary and idiom of the region. Heaney in this and successive works, *Door into the Dark* (1969), *Wintering Out* (1972), *North* (1976) and in his most recent book, *The Haw Lantern* (1987), traces the

effects of Ulster history. It is an attempt to give poetic expression to the historical unease that troubles the province, and which over the last twenty years has erupted into violence. The bog has become a kind of symbol of history into which has sunk settler and native, Protestant and Catholic, Planter and Gael. From time to time clues of this past are unearthed to remind the reader of the 'hidden' world that has been

suppressed, conquered, half assimilated. Heaney's approach to the fragmented and adversarial culture of Ulster is equivocal:

———————

I am neither internee nor informer;
An inner emigre, grown long-haired
And thoughtful; a wood-kerne

Escaped from the massacre,
Taking protective colouring
From bole and bark, feeling
Every wind that blows . . .

YEATS COUNTRY, COUNTY SLIGO

• OSCAR WILDE •

Oscar Fingal O'Flahertie Wills Wilde was the second son of very gifted parents. His father was a well-known eye-surgeon, a noted Irish antiquarian; and his mother was a society hostess and writer of verse in the Irish nationalist paper, *The Nation*. Wilde read classics at Trinity College, Dublin, and later at Oxford, where he took a double first and won the Newdigate prize for poetry. When he was twenty five he launched himself on London society as an asthete, wit, poet and provocative man of fashion. His first success was a lecture tour of the United States in 1882 where he brought to the raw West an appreciation of the finer points of Pre-Raphaelite painting and William Morris design. His progress in America was followed with almost as much interest by London correspondents as by frontier society.

During the course of the next few years he married, established a life style of comparative luxury through lecturing and as editor of *Woman's World*. He wrote a series of children's stories and published his first novel, *The Picture of Dorian Gray* in 1891. Within four years he had published the same number of plays – *Lady Windermere's Fan*, *A Woman of No Importance*, *The Ideal Husband* and *The Importance of Being Earnest* – light comedies of sparkling wit which conquered the London stage.

His self-confidence, his deliberate flaunting of society's conventions, his amoral – but in fact compassionate – attitudes which can be seen in essays like *The Soul of Man under Socialism* – delighted the public and outraged conventional opinion. And when Wilde's liaison with a Lord Alfred Douglas, the son of the Marquis of Queensbury, took these attitudes from the confines of the stage into society life, they exposed Wilde to humiliation and imprisonment. Having been provoked into issuing libel proceedings against the Marquis, Wilde lost the case and, on the basis of certain admissions he made during the trial, found himself facing criminal prosecution for homosexual offences. He was found guilty and sentenced to two years hard labour. During his imprisonment he wrote *De Profundis*, an apologia for his actions; and, after his release, *The Ballad of Reading Gaol*. Deprived of his position in public life, branded a criminal and corrupter of youth, his last sad years, bereft of health, wealth and reputation, were spent in Paris, where he died on November 30th, 1900.

not fit conveniently into neat categories. The finest example of this is Joyce's *Ulysses*, which does not seek to represent merely the life of an individual or even of a group, but of a whole city. In the contemporary period the focus of political writing has shifted to the north of Ireland, where problems are frequently obscured by the reliance on apparently simple labels – Catholic and Protestant, nationalist and unionist. The writers constantly prick our intelligence by pointing to the complexities which hide behind such labels. Seamus Heaney, from a rural, Catholic background, writes poetry which is concerned with delving, digging and uncovering. His object is to bring to light matters which we might prefer to remain hidden. He is not simply trying to see both sides; rather his poetry is a recognition and a reminder of the multi-faceted nature of the north's problems. For Roman Catholic and nationalist readers, Heaney's poetry is a description of their experience which refuses to dismiss complexity. For Protestant and unionist readers, it is a revelation of the richness of experience which they would be foolhardy to reject. Heaney's poetry is balanced by the urban, Protestant poetry of Tom Paulin. Heaney's poetry is dominated by images of digging; Paulin, in his exasperated, sometimes outraged, yet often affectionate examination of the north's Protestant traditions, writes poems in which images of frontiers and borders abound. Appalled by the arbitrariness of borders – they are just 'lines on the grass' – he is also keenly aware of their powerful constraining influence. For Paulin the enemy is narrowness, for Heaney shallowness; both writers taken together, show how it is possible to go beyond the confines and constraints of entrenched political attitudes.

Irish writers have over the years placed their work into the centre of Irish life. Without the so-called 'Literary Revival' at the beginning of the century Irish claims to nationhood would have been weaker. Without the literary conscience supplied by writers after the Civil War Irish society would have been even more oppressive. Without the political intelligence of contemporary writers the northern problem would be much less comprehensible. While steadfastly dealing with the specifics of Irish existence, the writers have made a case for the necessity of literature for the health of a society. Literature is not just something to turn to for escapist pleasure; it is also a powerful medium of political self-expression when other, more overt, channels are closed down. The experience of Irish literature stands as a powerful and heartening example for people in very different circumstances, showing, as it does, that it is possible for a people to shape its political and cultural destiny.

COMMUNITY

The appeal of Irish writing is based on its ability to make specific Irish details relevant to others. Irish literature is the literature of a small island and it derives much of its strength from that fact. All Irish writers are aware of the tight-knit communities from which they come. This sense of community is rare in modern life; more usual is the alienation felt by inhabitants of large cities. To some extent the writing of the Literary Revival was based on the hope of rescuing a sense of community from the onslaught of the modern world; it was a search of an ideal society in which all lives are meaningfully united. Irish writing offers a vision of what life might be if one could structure society around the idea of community. At the same time the modernity of Ireland and Irish writing must be acknowledged. In Ireland, too, alienation from the community is a commonplace of existence. To remain within the community it is necessary to conform. But Irish writing is not conformist, and the experience of the Irish writer, often reflected in his work, is the experience of alienation made all the more painful by the fact that a strong community spirit still exists.

Yeats' ideal of a 'Unity of Culture' was based on the hope that Irish culture could bring together all classes of people into one community. But Yeats knew that communities could exist only in small local forms, not in a single national entity. Joyce's work returns again and again to the artist's need to cut himself off from the conformity of the community in order to develop, but it also returns to the fact that the artist needs the community in order to develop properly. The novels and the plays of Beckett present us with characters whose existence is solitary and therefore meaningless; their only hope lies in the recourse to storytelling, since stories must be told to someone else. If solitude is a cause of regret for Beckett's characters, it is something to be striven for in the works of Francis Stuart, one of Ireland's oddest and most underrated novelists. From the start of his career Stuart has attempted to escape from what he perceives as the false hope of community into a marginal existence where he can develop fully as a writer. Even Stuart, however, has to acknowledge that the wish to develop as an artist springs from the desire to instruct the people in truths which are impossible to understand unless the artist stands outside the conformist constraints of community.

Irish writing has much to offer in the way of fine writing, humour and passion. They are evident to all who read it. More important, Irish literature proves that it is possible for poems, stories and plays to have an impact upon life.

· FRANCIS STUART ·

Stuart is one of the most controversial and intriguing of Irish literary characters. Born in Australia and educated at English public school, he has lived most of his life in Ireland. As a young man he married Iseult the daughter of Maud Gonne, who of course was the subject of so much of Yeats' love poetry.

Francis Stuart believed that the writer had to engross himself in human degradation in order to be inspired to write. He lived in Parisian brothels in the 1930s and Nazi Germany during the Second World War, where he worked as a broadcaster. As a result of this last activity, Stuart was interned at the end of the war by the allies. As he himself admitted he had "gone beyond the pale". Later he returned to Ireland, where he still lives. His stunning autobiography, *Blacklist Section* H, is one of the most extraordinary pieces of writing to come out of Ireland this century.

· EDNA O'BRIEN ·

Edna O'Brien was born in the west of Ireland and now lives in London. Beginning with The Country Girls, first published in 1960, she has written a succession of very successful novels and short stories. Kingsley Amis attributed to that first success 'an unphoney charm and unlaborious originality.' This novel and later ones are set in the Ireland of her own girlhood; there is a nostalgia and a kind of anguish in them which never descends into sentimentality. The first experiences of two young girls in the 'big city' is perhaps as good an example as any:

We got ready quickly and went down into the neon fairyland of Dublin. I loved it more than I had ever loved a summer's day in a hayfield. Lights, faces, traffic, the enormous vitality of people hurrying to somewhere. A dark-faced woman, in an orange silk thing, went by. 'Christ, they're in their underwear here,' Baba said.

IRISH MUSIC

The pipe band in the green and gold attract
a small following in Aughrim, County
Wicklow.

116

From the early days of Gaelic society to the present, music has played a major role in Irish life; and while the cities and towns of Ireland may now resound to the universal sounds of mass popular culture and music, there is nevertheless a genuine awareness among Irish people of the strength and importance of Irish traditional music and song. The music of Ireland represents a deep repository of a shared culture, created by the common people over the centuries. Its richness and subtlety reflects the spirit of an ancient people, and the poetry and imagery of the songs reflect the hopes and aspirations and disappointments of a country whose history has been often troubled and tragic.

One of the best ways to get to know Ireland is to attend one of the music sessions which are frequently held in pubs and bars. Often the best sessions, with the best music, are to be found in the most unprepossessing of bars; so do not be put off by appearances, and do not be afraid to talk to the neighbours on either side of you, for that too is all part of the 'crack'. In some of the cities and towns there are music sessions put on for the benefit of tourists, but these tend to be either stage-Irish or schmaltzy and should be avoided.

Just as Ireland's history has been greatly influenced by its geographical position on the western extremities of Europe, so too has its music. Numerous invaders and migrants arrived from Europe to this last outpost and stayed there with their cultures, thereby influencing and changing Ireland's development. Yet Ireland was outside the mainstream of European development and was less influenced by developments on the continent than other countries. Geographical remoteness, combined with the general cultural attitudes engendered by Ireland's social and political history, have meant the survival of a music which might otherwise have been lost, of a musical tradition which can be traced back to the medieval period. In one sense, therefore, Ireland's isolation has been a blessing in disguise.

The advance of industrialization in the 19th and early 20th centuries contributed to the virtual disappearance of traditional music in many parts of the world. Yet this process largely by-passed Ireland, which retained much of its traditional rural culture. During the period of English conquest and colonization in the 17th and 18th centuries, there arose a great division between the Protestant government and aristocracy, on the one hand, and the Roman Catholic common people, who were overwhelmingly peasants, on the other. There were the political differences between conquerors and conquered and the

RIGHT *A young piper at the annual Irish festival in London; music plays a crucial role in developing a cultural identity in expatriate Irish communities.*

ABOVE FAR RIGHT *A woodcut showing the origins of the pipes on the battlefield; a piper leads these 16th century foot soldiers. The bagpipe he plays has two drones and a very long chanter (the pipe and reed upon which the tune is played).*

BELOW FAR RIGHT *In America ballads about the homeland and about the experience of emigration were often included in musical shows and later sold as sheet music, like the sad and sentimental tale of Pat Molloy, 'The Irish Emigrant'.*

obscure stringed instrument about which little is known). While bagpipes of various sorts were common instruments in many parts of Europe, the harp became particularly associated with Ireland – indeed it still is, having become, with the shamrock, one of the national emblems of the island. Ireland is remarkable in being one of the few countries to have a musical instrument as its national emblem, and it appears on coinage as early as the reign of King Henry VI during the 15th century.

One of the first descriptions of Irish instrumental music is to be found in the writings of the Welsh-born chronicler of the Normans, Giraldus Cambrensis (Gerald Barry), who came to Ireland after the Norman invasion of 1169. Although he disliked the native Irish for what he considered to be their general laziness and barbarian habits, he noted that Irish harpers were much more skilful than any he had heard on the continent.

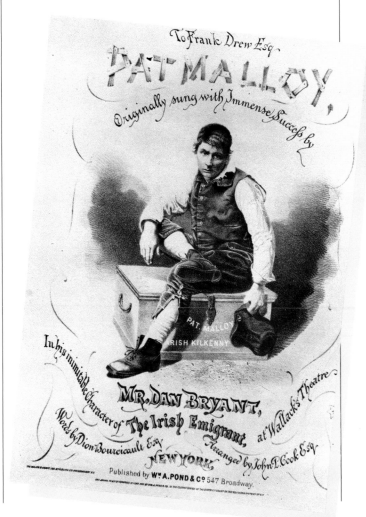

social differences between a small aristocratic and merchant class and a large number of peasants and urban poor. While the nobility had the time and money and power to promote and pursue all the arts of literature, painting and 'high' music (during a most important formative period for European music), the peasantry had many fewer opportunities for self-expression; they had not the education for literature and they lacked the time and money for the other arts. Except music. It was through music played on cheap instruments that the common people expressed themselves, singing songs about their lives and dancing their cares away. The peasantry proclaimed its worth in song. For a long time it was the only way for poor people to record their lives and history; until comparatively recently only the lives and deeds of the rich and powerful were felt to be worth recording.

The folk music of the common people was played at wakes and weddings, fairs and festivals and other social gatherings in village and town. During the 18th and 19th centuries many Irish people felt alienated from the English or Anglo-Irish domination of official life and the culture that went with it. They maintained their traditional social entertainments, in which music, song and dance played a major role.

In the Middle Ages the three most important Irish musical instruments were the harp, the bagpipes and the 'tiompan' (an

118

• FESTIVAL DANCER •

I find among the people considerable diligence only on musical instruments, on which they are incomparably more skilled than any nation I have seen. Their style is not, as on British instruments to which we are accustomed, deliberate and solemn, but quick and lively; nevertheless the sound is smooth and pleasant. It is remarkable that, with such a quick fingerwork, the musical rhythm is maintained and that, by unfailingly disciplined art, the integrity of the tune is fully preserved throughout the ornate rhythms and profusely intricate polyphony.

The music of the harp was an integral part of Irish life and of that Gaelic civilization which had given so much to Europe. Sir Francis Bacon wrote in 1627: 'no harp hath the sound so melting and prolonged as the Irish harp'. The oldest known Irish harp is the so-called 'Brian Boru Harp' preserved in Trinity College, Dublin, which dates from the fourteenth century; it is one of the few musical instruments which have survived intact from medieval Europe.

Irish music flourished for four hundred years under the patronage of the aristocracy and noble families, and indeed of the Norman conquerors, many of whom became 'more Irish than the Irish'. Since that music depended on an elaborate form of aristocratic patronage, and was by all accounts refined and decorous, and rarely danced to, it cannot be called folk music. Nor, indeed, was the harp at this time a folk instrument. The court poets, like the harpers, occupied an honoured place in Gaelic life and were accorded a high social status. The poems were composed for the members of noble families, in praise of kings and chiefs, and were written in a highly stylized manner; they were sung or recited to the accompaniment of the harp. While much of the poetry was written down and preserved, virtually no written evidence of the music remains; nor have any of the melodies survived orally.

The beginning of the 17th century marked a vital turning point in Irish history. The Battle of Kinsale in 1601 gave the English forces of Queen Elizabeth a decisive victory over the Irish, a victory which signalled the beginning of the end for the old Gaelic society. English administration, laws and practices were effectively applied to the whole of Ireland for the first time. The Cromwellian conquest some 50 years later brought about the final collapse of Gaelic Ireland.

As part of the process of destroying the Gaelic way of life, and securing the English subjection of Ireland, the harpers and poets were outlawed. Queen Elizabeth herself gave orders 'to hang the harpers wherever found', and though the law was frequently not carried out to the letter, during the 17th century they were proscribed and persecuted; they risked the death sentence and there were severe penalties for anyone harbouring them. During the Cromwellian rule of the mid-17th century, all harpers, pipers and wandering musicians had to obtain identity cards in the form of government permits before being allowed to travel through the country. It became common official practice to burn harps wherever they were found. In the early 19th century Thomas Moore wrote a song which became famous in Ireland, lamenting the loss of the music.

ABOVE LEFT *An elegant study in concentration at an Irish feis (festival), but not in Ireland; the competing dancers are American.*

LEFT *No pennies for a penny whistle, Dublin; the city teems with street buskers.*

The harp that once, thro' Tara's halls,
The soul of music shed,
Now hangs as mute on Tara's walls,
As if that soul were fled;
So sleeps the pride of former days,
So glory's thrill is o'er;
And hearts, that once beat high for praise,
Now feel that pulse no more.

From around 1600 a major change began to occur in the structure of music in England and in continental Europe, and this was a new system of music based on major and minor keys rather than on 'modes' (the scale of each mode starts on a different note, so that the semitones fall in different places in each). The new scales became the norm in Europe, and by the 18th century modal music was rarely practised. This did not happen in Ireland. Musicians continued to make their music in the only way they knew, in the modes, so that the old music became a form of memory and lament for an age which had passed and provided a kind of cultural resistance to the alien manners of the English conquerors.

As the old Gaelic order disintegrated, the court poets and harpers lost their social status and livelihoods. Much Irish poetry and song of the 17th and 18th centuries laments this loss of position and the decline of the great Roman Catholic families. One example of this genre is the 'Lament for Kilcash' (right), a castle in County Tipperary, one of the chief seats of the Butler family: with the cutting down of the forests comes the loss of the old hunting grounds, and the passing of the old Gaelic order.

The harpers became itinerant musicians, travelling the countryside, composing and playing music to whomever would listen and pay for it, or would provide food, drink and general hospitality. Many of these travelling harpers were blind, and the harping technique survived partly because it was one of the few ways in which a blind man could make a living. Most of their tunes have been lost, and we know little detail of their lives, except for one, Carolan, the last and most famous of the harper-composers.

He was born in 1670 and had the good fortune to fall under the patronage of Mrs MacDermott Roe, whose husband was head of one of the historic families of Connaught. After Carolan was blinded by smallpox at the age of 18, she had him taught the harp so that he could make a living for himself, and when after three years he had completed his studies, she provided him with a horse, a guide and money. For almost 50 years, until his death in 1738, Carolan travelled the length and breadth of Ireland, staying at the houses of his patrons. He was different from the other travelling musicians in that he had a remarkable gift for composition; he composed many melodies for the men and women who offered him hospitality, as well as verses to suit the tunes. Carolan's fame spread throughout Ireland, and the beauty of his music has remained with us, more than 200 of his melodies having been preserved (many more have undoubtedly been lost). He was influenced by the Italian composers, such as Geminiani and Vivaldi, who were much in vogue in Dublin, and he succeeded in some of his airs in marrying, in a manner enchanting to the ear, historic Irish music with early 18th-century Italian music. At the age of 68, after a lifetime of music and travelling, he returned to the house of his aged patroness, Mrs MacDermott Roe. On his death-bed he took up his harp one last time, and played the sad and lovely melody, 'Carolan's Farewell to Music'.

What shall we do for timber?
The last of the woods is down,
Kilcash and the house of its glory
And the bell of the house are gone;
The spot where that lady waited
Who shamed all women for grace,
When earls came sailing to greet her
And Mass was said in the place.

My grief and my affliction
Your gates are taken away,
Your avenue needs attention;
Goats in the garden stray;
The courtyard's filled with water
And the great earls where are they?
The earls, the lady, the people
Beaten into the clay.

Despite the success and fame of Carolan, the harping tradition was on the verge of extinction. The great Harp Festival held in Belfast in 1792 was one attempt to revive it, but of the 10 harpers present, only a blind harper from Derry, Denis Hempson, aged 97, still played the harp in the traditional manner, using his long finger nails to pluck the wire-strung harp. The old harping tradition then died out, and although there were renewed attempts made to revive it at the end of the next century, the tradition had been lost, and the frail link which joined the travelling musicians of the 18th century to the Gaelic harpers of the 12th century irrevocably broken.

Before 1800 the Irish language was the spoken tongue of most people, and the songs and poetry were composed in the native tongue. Love songs were the most common, many of them betraying a French influence derived from the Normans. Great numbers of these Gaelic songs and verses were noted down by scholars and collectors in the 18th and 19th centuries, but unfortunately few noted the airs to which they were sung. As a result, many of them were put to other airs, either traditional Irish ones or English or Scottish ones.

The old Gaelic order, which had started to disintegrate with the defeat at Kinsale in 1601, received its death blow from the victory of William of Orange over the Stuart king, James II at the Battle of the Boyne in 1690. The Gaelic poets clung to the hope of a Stuart restoration to the English throne, believing that to contain the only chance of a national revival in Ireland. They invented a new literary device in the 18th century, the *aisling* or vision poetry, in which the poet in a dream meets a beautiful woman in distress, who is mourning a lost hero or lover. Either he comforts the lady and promises her redress, or she tells him that she is grieving from the oppression of foreigners who will soon be driven out by the return of a Stuart king and by help from abroad. The beautiful woman, of course, is Ireland, but because poets and musicians were seen by the state as dangerous people, they avoided using the name of Ireland in song. Overtly nationalist folk songs in Gaelic are comparatively few. The poets used the device of giving secret love names to their country, names such as Cathleen Ni Houlihan, Granuaile, Dark Rosaleen, or Roisin Dubh ('Little Black Rose').

By the 18th century the most popular instruments were the Irish pipes and the fiddle. These pipes derived from the old mouth-blow war pipes, which had been used widely in Ireland and elsewhere for centuries before. The newer form of the pipes were elbow-blown. They are called 'uileann' (Irish for 'elbow') or union pipes. The bag is filled by a bellows attached

RIGHT The footwork of traditional Irish dance is intricate and energetic; attention is focused on the movement of the feet by the lack of any arm movement. Some forms of traditional Scottish dance are similar.

• THE IRISH HARP •

The small portable harp used by the medieval minstrels to entertain the chiefs of Ireland has, like the shamrock and the wolfhound, long been used as an official symbol of the nation. It was usually represented in gold on a blue ground – St Patrick's blue – and in its original form survives today only on the personal flag of the President of Ireland and on the Royal Arms of Britain where it was first established in the reign of James I. Henry VIII minted a groat in 1526 which was the first use of the harp on coinage, and in the nineteenth century the poet Thomas Moore lamented the decline of Gaelic Ireland in popular poems such as 'The Harp the once through Tara's Hall', while the painter Daniel MacLeise made liberal use of the harp in many political and historical decorations to symbolize Ireland. Most of his paintings show a style of instrument similar to the 'Brian Boru' harp, made some time between the 13th and the 16th century and now housed in Trinity College, Dublin. The fact that this instrument was adopted as the symbol of the Guinness brewery in 1862, and was incorporated into the Irish coinage in 1926, further ensured its familiarity as Ireland's symbol.

FAR LEFT *A magnificent Irish harp fashioned by Colm O'Meacher in the Marley Craft Courtyard, Dublin.*

LEFT *A Unionist recruiting poster of 1862 for the American Civil War; shamrocks – and the ever-emotive image of the harp – used to attract men to the Irish regiment forming in New York.*

TOP RIGHT *James Galway, the celebrated Irish flautist, often plays with the Chieftains, and like them, has long been an effective ambassador for traditional Irish music.*

RIGHT *Ulsterman Derek Bell of the Chieftains; not only a superb harpist, he plays piano, oboe, cor anglais and dulcimer. His long interest in traditional Irish instruments led to his reconstruction of the ancient Irish timpan.*

CORCORAN LEGION
FIFTH REGIMENT.
COL. WILLIAM McEVILY

A FEW GOOD MEN ARE WANTED
TO FILL UP CAPT. WM. L. MONEGAN'S COMPANY.
This is a splendid opportunity for young men to join a Crack Regiment. You will have good officers, who will pay every attention to your welfare.

All Promotions will be made from the Ranks!
Relief Tickets will be immediately issued to Families of Volunteers.
The highest Bounties will be paid, and good Quarters, Rations and Uniforms furnished.
This Regiment is quartered at STATEN ISLAND, in a position highly favorable to the health and good condition of the men.
THOSE WISHING TO JOIN CAN APPLY TO   Recruiting Officers.
Lieuts. MICHAEL McDONALD, and
DANIEL H. McDONNELL,
No. 52 FIRST AVE. COR. OF THIRD ST.

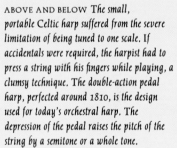

ABOVE AND BELOW The small, portable Celtic harp suffered from the severe limitation of being tuned to one scale. If accidentals were required, the harpist had to press a string with his fingers while playing, a clumsy technique. The double-action pedal harp, perfected around 1810, is the design used for today's orchestral harp. The depression of the pedal raises the pitch of the string by a semitone or a whole tone.

124

to the arm; a chanter or melody pipe gives a two-octave range, and a set of three drones provides a continuous, unchanging accompaniment to the chanter. There are also three regulators, or keys, on the drones, from which simple chords can be played to accompany the melody by depressing the wrist. It is a most complex and difficult instrument, and tradition has it that it takes seven years of practice and seven more years of playing before one can think of oneself as a piper. Yet when one hears a master of the pipes, such as Liam O'Flynn, the haunting beauty and uniqueness of the sound produced cannot fail to leave a deep and moving impression.

The fiddle had been accepted by the ordinary people by the 17th century. An Englishman, Richard Head, wrote in 1674 of Sunday pastimes in Ireland: 'in every field a fiddle and the lasses footing it until they are all of a foam'.

Much Irish instrumental music is dance music. The absence of any references to dancing in medieval Irish literature has led some people to believe that there was little dancing in Gaelic Ireland. But this seems most unlikely, given the musical achievements of the Irish at that time and the customs of Celtic people elsewhere in Europe. What is certain is that by the late 17th and early 18th centuries dancing had become a craze. One writer recorded in 1728 that:

Even the very lame and blind,
If trump or bagpipe they do hear,
In dancing posture do appear.

In the late 1770s, Arthur Young wrote of his tour in Ireland:

Dancing is very general among the poor people, almost universal in every
cabbin. Dancing-masters of their own rank travel through the country from
cabbin to cabbin, with a piper or blind fiddler; and the pay is sixpence a
quarter. It is an absolute system of education. Weddings are always celebrated
with much dancing; and a Sunday rarely passes without a dance.

The surviving folk dances are the jig, the hornpipe and the reel, along with various set dances. Most of the dances owe their form and steps to the dancing masters who toured the countryside teaching new dances to an eager audience. The arrival of the dancing master at a village was an occasion of great delight, for it meant six weeks of music, dancing and gaiety. Despite the oppression and poverty of rural Ireland in the 18th century, the spirit and gaiety of the common people

LEFT *Street busker, Kilkenny.*

ABOVE *Traditional music at Siamsa Cottage, Finuge in County Kerry.*

found expression in music and dance. The dances were usually held on the village green or at a crossroads, and the tradition continued well into the late 19th century. However, after the Great Famine of the 1840s, there was a drastic decline in music and dancing, due partly to the Famine's terrible impact on social life and the subsequent emigration, partly to the puritanical efforts of some members of the Catholic clergy, who regarded dance meetings as sinful. Most of the dance music was composed in the 18th century and it is a tribute to its high quality, despite the almost complete replacement of traditional by modern dancing, that so much of it has survived.

The defeat of the United Irishmen's rebellion in 1798 and the Act of Union of 1801, which abolished the Irish parliament, put an end for some time to Irish nationalist aspirations. This was a period which inspired the production of many patriotic and revolutionary songs, such as 'The Boys of Wexford' and 'The Croppy Boy'. The big difference was that these songs were written in English, whereas down to the close of the 18th century the vast majority of people spoke little or no English and had sung in their native language. But the Irish language was being replaced by English, and after the Famine, which hit particularly hard the poorer Gaelic-speaking regions, Irish came to be regarded as a language for the backward, hindering progress. Moreover, the English and Scottish settlers, soldiers returning from wars, and the seasonal migration of labourers to England and Scotland all increased the flow of English and Scottish folk songs into the country. And as well there were Anglo-Irish folk songs, songs written by Irishmen in English.

The early years of the 19th century saw the appearance of the street singer or ballad singer. He sang at fairs and rural gatherings, selling the broadsheets which carried the texts of his songs. He sang in a strong voice, pitched as high as possible, so as to make himself heard over the noise of the throng. There were ballads on every subject, from courtship to politics, recording events of local history or of national importance. They were altered and reshaped by individual singers to suit local taste. Many songs in English were, in fact, adapted to be sung to authentic Gaelic airs. Traditions overlap, so that it is often impossible to be sure of the origins of either the music or the words of a song. Variation is always present the same tune or song is performed by different musicians and singers in different ways; the same tune may have many different titles; and for dance music, the names have no musical connection whatever with the tunes, being merely labels, as in 'The Mason's Apron', 'Drowsy Maggie' or 'The Hare in the Corn'.

The disappearance of Irish as the vernacular in the 19th century, and the eroding of many old customs, raised the danger that many of the old melodies would be lost forever. Fortunately, beginning with Edward Bunting in the 1790s, there appeared a handful of men who for the next 100 years undertook the systematic collection of melodies and songs from all over Ireland, going out into the countryside to write down the tunes from traditional musicians and singers wherever they could be found. In the words of one of them, George Petrie, it was his duty 'to preserve the native melodies, because of a deep sense of their beauty, a strong sense of their archaeological interest and a desire to aid in the preservation of remains so honourable to the national character of the country'. Thanks to men like him, some of the most beautiful airs in Irish music were kept alive, and the music and songs from their collections are often performed today.

In his 'Irish Melodies', published between 1808 and 1834, Thomas Moore changed many of these traditional airs to suit his own verses. His songs were sentimental and nostalgic, suited to the polite drawing-room society of Dublin and London, and they have been deplored by purists for destroying the rugged, primitive quality of the original music. William Hazlitt said that Moore had 'converted the wild harp of Erin into a musical snuff-box'. Yet songs such as 'Love Thee, Dearest', 'The Last Rose of Summer' and 'The Meeting of the Waters' came to be sung all over Ireland, and they still have a place of affection in many people's hearts. That most famous of Irish tenors, John McCormack, made them an important part of his repertoire and gave them great popularity in America.

The growth of the nationalist movement in the 19th and early 20th centuries inspired the composition of many patriotic ballads which vaunted the heroes of the past and were aimed at stirring up national pride and resistance. In their newspaper, The Nation, the leaders of the Young Ireland Movement published songs such as 'A Nation Once Again' and 'The Memory of the Dead', which immediately swept the country. The Times remarked that such songs were 'far more dangerous than O'Connell's speeches'. The Fenian rebellion of the 1860s, the 1916 Easter Rising and the war of independence between 1919 and 1921 gave rise to a host of rebel songs. Some were of dubious quality; others, like 'The Foggy Dew' and 'Kevin Barry' became standard pieces in houses and pubs all over Ireland.

In the 20th century, especially since 1945, modern pop and rock music have taken over in Ireland as they have in most other western countries.

At the end of 1984 the world turned its attentions to the magnitude of the human disaster caused by famine in Ethiopia. Human concern was one thing, action another; and one musician, Bob Geldof, set about organizing the greatest charity fundraising event in history. The first step was the release in December of that year of the single, 'Do they know it's Christmas?', co-written with Midge Ure and performed by some of the pop world's greatest talents. It became the biggest-selling single record in history. The culmination of the process that Geldof had started was the extraordinary event in the summer of 1985, when the Live Aid concert was staged concurrently in London and Philadelphia. It featured 52 acts, was watched on television in 500 million homes and raised a staggering 50 million pounds for famine relief in Ethiopia.

Geldof was the chief inspirer, planner and instigator at every stage of the operation. His collapse from nervous exhaustion during the Wembley concert was testimony to an effort which would have been beyond most human beings.

Geldof, who had been educated at Blackrock College, outside Dublin, had come to public attention thanks to the success of his group, the Boomtown Rats. The Rats, formed in Dun Laoghairie in 1975, rapidly became the Irish representatives of the punk 'new wave' which was sweeping through pop music. Songs such as 'Rat Trap', 'Looking after Number One' and 'I Don't Like Mondays' were major successes for the group, but their popularity was also based on the personality of Geldof himself. His rapport with his fans on stage was coupled with his articulate, irreverent style off it. He became a regular guest on chat shows on both sides of the Atlantic.

Yet few people would have believed, before 1984, that Bob Geldof, with his occasional flashes of bad language and uncombed hair, could possibly have within him the gift for moral leadership that would stir a whole generation of young people into raising millions of pounds for starving Africa.

The great humanitarian achievements of Geldof must not distract attention from his music. The Boomtown Rats fit into a definite genre of music, with the addition of a distinctive Irish ingredient. Central to this style is a rawness characteristic of all Irish rock music; there is an energy, derived partly from the lack of synthetic packaging, at the heart of the music's appeal. Take, for example, one of the greatest white blues singers around, Belfast-born and bred Van Morrison. Van has been around for so long that it is difficult to believe that he is only in his early forties. His survival is remarkable. His breakthrough came in the mid-1960s, when the blues were at their popular height, but his

· THE CHIEFTAINS ·

The Chieftains are the most famed of all traditional Irish music groups. They were first formed in 1963 and since then have always been under the musical directorship of Paddy Moloney, whose commitment to traditional music has never wavered. What marked out the group back in the 1960s, at a time when interest in folk-oriented music was widespread, was its exploration of traditional instrumental music. While other Irish singing groups and individual singers have attracted international attention, the Chieftains have filled the Albert and Carnegie Halls, as *Time* magazine noted 'not because they are Irish but because they sing no songs and instead spin out purified instrumentals of the reel, jig, slide, Kerry Polka and other such traditional forms.'

Not surprisingly during such a long period of touring and recording, there have been several changes of personnel: the flautist Matt Molloy, pictured here, joined the group in 1979. In 1975 the group won an Oscar for the film score of Stanley Kubrick's *Barry Lyndon* and in 1983 toured China.

appeal is still strong today when many of his contemporaries have faded away. Morrison's talent has been the strength of his voice.

Listen to his early hit, 'Brown-eyed Girl', or to the later 'St Dominic's Preview', and his sustained popularity, both in Europe and the United States, will become clear.

Van Morrison has been, above all, a survivor, through more than 20 years of recording and gigging. Sadly, the same cannot be said of Phil Lynott, leader of the highly successful and influential group Thin Lizzy. The death of this talented musician in January, 1986, robbed rock music of the driving force behind one of Ireland's most impressive bands, a fine, hard-rocking group who were equally at home with softer blues ballads. It was also one of the most exciting bands to be seen live. Best known for the rock version of the classic folk tune, 'Whiskey in the Jar', which was its first hit, the group continued with such classics as 'The Boys are Back in Town' and 'Waiting for an Alibi'. In all they enjoyed nine top-ten hits in the United Kingdom and also some success in the United States.

The rough edge which has become a hallmark of Irish rock music has always been prominent in the work of the two major bands to come out of the six counties since the re-emergence of the Troubles in the late 1960s. From the Protestant side of the community came Stiff Little Fingers, formed in Belfast in 1977. Led by the charismatic Jake Burns, the group seemed destined for the top, with a string of exciting albums. Their closeness to their roots and their ability to write songs with both a strong political and personal message promised great success; but it never really came and they split up in 1983. From the other side of the divide came the Undertones, a Derry group which was to enjoy great commercial success in the United Kingdom. The lead singer, Feargal Sharkey, whose quavering voice was the hallmark of the group, later embarked on a highly successful solo career.

The appeal of those two groups was a shade parochial. The same cannot be said of U2. By the mid-1980s this group had conquered America and was being called the greatest rock-and-roll band in the world. Formed in Dublin in 1979, it has managed to combine high-energy rock with lyrics containing an unusually high level of political and social comment. U2, especially the lead singer, Bono, have become virtual spokesmen for a new generation of Irish youth. The Croke Park concert of 1987, which followed a hugely successful tour of America, was the social event of the year in Ireland. There is no reason to doubt that U2 will go from strength to strength. It can justly claim to be Ireland's greatest-ever rock band.

Despite the commercial dominance of pop music traditional music has lived on, most strongly in small farming areas, and a great debt is owed to the musicians who have kept it alive at a time when the past is being rejected in favour of anything modern.

Since the 1960s there has been a remarkable upsurge of interest in traditional music. This is partly due to the influence of Comhaltas Ceoltoiri Eireann (Irish Music Society), established in 1951, which among other things organizes a large festival of traditional music ('fleadh cheoil') every year in a small town in Ireland. It attracts a huge following and there are numerous other music festivals, especially during the summer months. The widespread popularity of ballad groups such as the Clancy Brothers and the Dubliners increased the interest in Irish music in the 1960s, a period when Irish youth were seeking for roots more solid than those provided by American and British pop music. Slowly, an awareness began to grow of the richness of Ireland's musical inheritance.

One of the most important figures in creating this awareness was Sean O'Riada, who took traditional airs and songs and treated them in a new exciting way. Traditional music had usually meant solo performance. O'Riada devised a means of group playing which actually strengthened its appeal. His Ceoltoiri Chualann were to become the now famous Chieftains group, and they were soon followed by other excellent groups, such as Planxty, the Bothy Band and De Danann. The popularity of the music played by these groups spread to many countries in Europe and to America.

Much more recently, Shaun Davy has composed music for the uileann pipes and full orchestra and has written modern music based on traditional themes. 'The Brendan Voyage' and 'Granuaile' are two such compositions which have won wide critical acclaim and brought Irish music to the attention of many who might otherwise have ignored it.

The rich store of Irish music and the skills of its musicians represent a tenuous and precious link with a tradition that stretches back over 1,000 years. Without it Irish culture would be lacking an integral part of its own particular genius. The music reflects the countryside and its people; the haunting sadness of the slow airs and laments mixes easily with the vitality and exhilaration of the reels. The strange, startling beauty of traditional Irish music is open to all who wish to discover it, and through it better understanding of the soul of its people and their history.

RIGHT *Bob Geldof, one of the most famous popular musicians in the world; but not, primarily, for his music.*

• BOB GELDOF •

SPORTING IRELAND

Stephen Roche and Sean Kelly. These two
great cyclists have been responsible for
popularizing their sport in Ireland. Roche's
victory in the 1987 Tour de France turned
him into a national hero. After winning
this event, previously monopolized by
continental Europeans, who could begrudge
him the extraordinary welcome he received
on his return to Dublin?

Two days before the end of the 1987 Tour de France cycling classic the Irish prime minister, Charles Haughey, made it known that he would be in Paris for the finish to greet fellow-Dubliner, Stephen Roche, in his hour of glory. Some cynics saw it as a shrewd political move, but it was a typically sporting gamble as well. Two days is a long time in the Tour de France and if Stephen Roche had failed to deliver the prime minister would have had egg on his face.

Of course, Roche did win the Tour de France to add to his Tour of Italy success; and after he won the World Professional Championship in August his native Dublin made him a freeman of the city. More than 20,000 people turned out to honour Roche in the city's first open-air ceremony of its kind. In receiving this accolade Roche followed in the footsteps of Pope John Paul II, President John F. Kennedy, Eamon de Valera and other renowned world figures.

Roche and his fellow-countryman, Sean Kelly of Tipperary, have put Ireland on the world cycling map in recent years. To the youth of Ireland they have given new meaning to the phrase 'on your bike'.

(Interestingly, although Ireland was not among the leading cycling nations until the arrival of Roche and Kelly, the country had produced an earlier world champion in Harry Reynolds, of Balbriggan, County Dublin, who won a world championship on the track in Copenhagen in 1896.)

The honours conferred on Roche are an indication of how deeply the Irish enjoy their sport and appreciate their sporting heroes. Even in grim economic times the level of public interest never wavers and it is often when things are at their worst that a sporting saviour is found to rekindle national morale. There was Ronnie Delany, who shocked the world by winning the Olympic 1,500 metres title at Melbourne in 1956. After he had crossed the line in victory he went on his knees to say a prayer of thanksgiving and his gesture prompted many a depressed Irish household of those hungry years to believe that they had a lot to be thankful for after all.

In Ireland the adulation of sports heroes is encouraged from early school days, when the athletic feats of strength and bravery of legendary figures like Cuchulainn and Fionn Mac-Cumhail provide a spectacular introduction to history studies. In practical terms, most Irish schoolchildren, especially boys, encounter sport for the first time through the games of the Gaelic Athletic Association. The GAA was founded more than a

LEFT *The experiment of combining Gaelic football and Australian Rules football produced a very entertaining hybrid sport which was tried out in the 1980s; Ireland's Spillane and Australia's Sailsbury are seen here at Croke Park. Both sports require strength, speed and skill and it is hoped that Ireland versus Australia will now become a regular fixture, despite the over-aggressive first few encounters between the two countries.*

century ago to cater for athletics, Gaelic football, hurling and handball and to provide an organized alternative to the games of the ruling British class.

Intensely national in concept, the GAA made it clear that its games were for the Irish only. Its structure was based on local clubs in every county and it was inter-club competition which gave the GAA its unrivalled position as the country's leading sports organization.

Battling for the honour of the little village in Gaelic football and hurling competition replaced the faction-fighting of former years, but the rivalry remained tribal and deep-rooted. The smouldering republicanism of the early years of this century had a friendly ally in the GAA, whose training fields were used as meeting places for the Volunteers throughout the country. Youngsters of that time now recall seeing men who shortly afterwards became heroes of the 1916 Rising and the Civil War training at local GAA fields under the pretext of being club members. In that way the Act of Unlawful Assembly was defeated and the British forces were hoodwinked.

The great majority of the Irish people were enthralled by the competitiveness and the robust nature of Gaelic games. Football, played with a soccer-type ball, allowed handling of the ball and frequent scoring. Fetching the ball high in the air and kicking points from long distances were the recognized skills of the game, but one had to be able to stand up to its physical, he-man elements as well. It had many of the best features of soccer and rugby, with none of the negative aspects, such as offside rules, time-wasting scrummaging and tactical touch-kicking.

Hurling, played with a hockey-stick-shaped implement made of ash (except that the end of the hurley is much bigger than the curved end of the hockey stick), is said to be the fastest and best field game in the world. The small, leather-bound ball is called a sliothar and can be hit vast distances either from the hand or from the ground.

As Gaelic games became organized throughout the country, interest in British field games diminished and those people who continued to play them were labelled 'West Brits', especially in rural areas. Playing British games involved fraternising with the occupiers of the country and the term 'West Brit' carried a stigma that lived on for generations, even among families who had long ceased to retain such links.

The early all-Ireland championships, or national championships, of the GAA were played on a club basis, but soon county organizations were formed and inter-county competition took

LEFT *Hurling, the gaelic sister of football, has become the more popular of the two sports in the 1980s. Said to be the fastest field sport in the world, there is no more spectacular sight than the all Ireland hurling final played each year at Croke Park.*

ABOVE *Liam Brady has been one of Ireland's greatest sporting ambassadors of late. This cultured midfield player possesses one of the most educated left feet in world soccer; and his skill, temperament and consistency have made him a favourite with the crowds in Ireland, Britain and Italy. His playing career has included spells with Arsenal, Inter Milan and Sampdoria. He is now back in England, playing for West Ham United.*

HORSE RACING

The Irish horse has a history going back some 600 years; it is recorded that Richard II, on his arrival in Ireland, was met by the king of Leinster, Art McMurrough Kavanagh, astride a magnificent white steed that 'without housing or saddle cost him 400 cows.' In 1673, Sir William Temple addressed a work entitled 'An Essay on the Advancement of Trade in Ireland' to the Lord Lieutenant, the Earl of Essex, urging the development of an export trade in horses. He noted that 'The soil is of a sweet and plentiful grass which will raise a large breed.' He was absolutely right, and the efforts of the Turf Club and the many superb Irish trainers – such as Paddy Prendergast and Vincent O'Brien – have attracted sufficient foreign investment to ensure the continued success of Irish-bred and trained horses throughout the world.

ABOVE RIGHT *Vincent O'Brien's training stables at Ballydoyle, County Tipperary.*

NEAR RIGHT *Races at Phoenix Park, a mile from the centre of Dublin, can be run either left-handed or right-handed; the track is particularly fast.*

RIGHT *Arkle, one of the greatest steeplechasers of all time, three-times winner of the Cheltenham Gold Cup, and 24 other races. His owner, Anne, the Duchess of Westminster, said she would never let him run in the Grand National 'because he was one of the family.'*

1 mile start

1 mile 1 furlong start

1 mile 2 furlong start

Winning Post

RIGHT *The charming paddock at Phoenix Park; a profusion of roses make this one of the most attractive courses. With 1,752 acres, Phoenix Park – the venue for the 1979 Papal Mass which attracted 1¼ million people – is certainly one of the largest parks in any European capital city.*

BELOW *The start of the 1987 Irish Derby at the Curragh; won by John Reid on Sir Harry Lewis.*

ABOVE Army officers preparing for a race in the dressing room at Punchestown.

BELOW The Illustrated Sporting and Dramatic News of October 1939 reports that 'Racing has been going on in neutral Eire much as usual'; Drumlargin won the main event for Mr Cuddy.

138

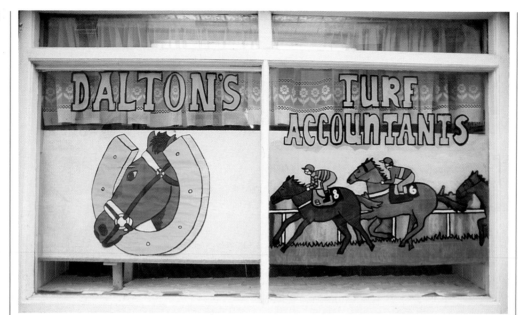

over. The all-Ireland championships begin with regional or provincial championships and the champions of Munster, Leinster, Connaught and Ulster qualify for the semi-finals. The four provincial champions play semi-finals, and all-Ireland final days, both in hurling and football, draw capacity attendances in the region of 70,000 to the GAA's headquarters at Croke Park, Dublin.

Kerry is the leading football county and has been the envy of the entire country for its ability to adapt to the evolving patterns of the game as the rules are modified and changed over the years. For instance, GAA teams at one time comprised 21 players, but this has been reduced to 15 for more than 70 years. Renowned for generations for its catch-and-kick style, Kerry proved equally adept when, in order to speed up the game, the rules were changed to put more emphasis on running and passing.

Down to the early 1970s the GAA operated a ban on what were termed 'foreign' games. These included rugby, soccer, hockey and cricket. It also banned members of the British forces from membership of the GAA. In the early 1970s, following strong campaigning from city-based clubs, the ban was removed and GAA members became free to play and attend the formerly banned games. The majority of players stayed loyal to Gaelic games, however, and the Association's position remained unchallenged.

Kerry's football dominance continued unbroken; the county enjoyed its most successful spell between the years 1975

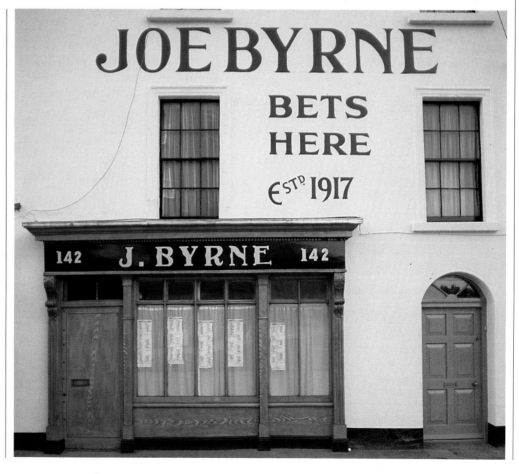

and 1986, during which it captured eight all-Ireland titles. The county has produced so many star players over the years that it is invidious to single out names from any generation, but mention must be made of five Kerrymen who share the record of having won all-Ireland medals in each of those years and head the list of individual medal holders. They are Mikey Sheehy, Ger Power, Ogie Moran, Paidi O Se and Pat Spillane.

Gaelic football history is rich in legendary names, from the Kildare stylist, Larry Stanley, of the 1920s, who was also an Olympic high jumper, to Mick O'Connell, a superb athlete from Valentia Island off the south Kerry coast, and the magnificent Sean Purcell from Galway, one of the most versatile players of all time.

Hurling is acknowledged as Ireland's uniquely national game, just as baseball belongs to the United States and cricket to England. A great many GAA players play both games at club level, but few make it to the top with their counties. Jack Lynch, of Cork, who became prime minister of Eire, was one of the few to win all-Ireland medals at both football and hurling and more recently another Corkman, Jimmy Barry Murphy, emulated him.

Cork leads the hurling honours list, and though it manages better than any other county to produce top-class teams in both hurling and football, hurling is its favourite game. The deeds of the mighty Christy Ring, the most famous hurler of all time, remain an inspiration to every young player who dons the county's red jersey. The jersey is tinged with white collar and cuffs, prompting a writer of the past to label it the 'Blood and Bandage' of Cork.

Christy Ring became the biggest name in hurling history, but Limerick people will forever claim that their own Mike Mackey, from Ahane, was the greatest. Mackey, with massive shoulders and powerful legs, topped by a close-cropped head of jet-black hair, was fearless in pursuit of the eliothar and unstoppable in full flight. Hurling has produced many other famous figures over the years, but Ring and Mackey remain the great folk heroes of the game and the arguments still go on as to which of them was the better.

Cork's hurling dominance has traditionally been challenged by their Munster rivals, Tipperary, and by Kilkenny, of Leinster. At one time it was every Tipperaryman's ambition to have Cork beaten and the hay saved before the end of July, but Tipperary have slumped during the past 15 years and the county is now engaged in a comprehensive, long-term, team-building effort to take it back to the top.

140

The GAA also caters for women. Camogie, which is hurling played on a slightly smaller pitch, and ladies football are the leading women's games. Cork, Kilkenny, Dublin and Antrim (in the north) produce great camogie teams and individuals almost every year, while the girls of Kerry seem to be in a class of their own at football. Handball remains immensely popular and the best Irish players compete with great success at international level in the United States and Canada.

Emigration having been such a persistent feature of Irish life, it is hardly surprising that Gaelic games should have prospered around the world, especially in Great Britain and the United States. In Great Britain the standard of inter-club competition is high and many second-generation Irish boys and girls play Gaelic games there with great success. New York is the strong base of the games in America, where the controversial Kerryman, John Kerry O'Donnell, hosts weekly games at his stadium, Gaelic Park, in the Bronx. O'Donnell has had a passionate interest in GAA affairs throughout his life and this passion has on many occasions spilled over into direct confrontation with the authorities in Dublin. New York's greatest GAA successes came in the mid-1950s, when many top-class Irish players left their native country to find work in the New World. New York could match any Irish county in football and hurling and scored a number of memorable wins against the best Irish sides, to the chagrin of the old country. Those days may soon return. Chicago, Boston and San Francisco have also built up strong GAA bases and visits to those centres during the Irish off-season have become plum prizes for All-Star Irish players.

During the past few years efforts have been made to develop a compromise game between Australian football and Gaelic football and several international series have been held in both countries. The 'mix' did not work to the satisfaction of either side and the contests were notable for their viciousness and bad sportsmanship. The authorities in both countries seem determined, however, to persevere in the attempt for another couple of years at least.

Despite the troubles in the Six Counties, the GAA remains strong there, although Down, in 1960 and 1961, is the only northern county to have won an all-Ireland senior championship (Tyrone made a valiant bid to dethrone the football champions, Kerry, in 1986). Training, especially in dark spring and autumn evenings, is a hazardous occupation in the Six Counties. The British forces have taken over the GAA's playing facilities at Crossmaglen, County Armagh, and in other sensitive areas.

Thanks to the efforts of a few athletes of world class, who

ABOVE *Pat Eddery was born into racing. His father Jimmy, a top Irish jockey, had won the Irish Derby and Oaks, his uncle Con Eddery was a trainer, and his maternal grandfather, Jack Moylan, was a fine steeplechase rider. Pat's early recklessness – he was suspended four times as an apprentice – has been replaced by a shrewd and cool temperament which has brought him champion jockey status. Trainer Peter Walwyn said of him: 'After horses he has ridden appear to have hard races, they come back to me as if they have never had a race at all.'*

have kept Ireland on the map in international competition, there is still considerable interest in track and field athletics in Ireland, although the most promising youngsters invariably take up university scholarships in the United States at an early age. This, coupled with the advent of television, which has spoiled us into being satisfied only with the very highest standards, has brought about the demise of many traditional village sports events which used to be annual features of Irish life. Still, the feats of John Treacy, who won a silver medal in the Los Angles Olympics marathon and two successive world cross-country championships, and of Eamonn Coghlan, world 5,000-metres champion in Helsinki in 1983 and the greatest indoor runner in American athletics history, have delighted a whole generation of Irish athletics enthusiasts.

In many parts of the world the racehorse trainer, Vincent O'Brien, may well be Ireland's best-known sportsman. As racing spreads on the international level the O'Brien name is always to the forefront. From modest beginnings in his native Cork, where his father was a small-time trainer, Vincent O'Brien has built a racing empire at Ballydoyle, County Tipperary, that is the envy of nearly everyone in the racing world.

In his early years as a trainer O'Brien dominated the jumping scene in both Ireland and England, while dabbling in the more remunerative flat-racing events. By the mid-1950s he had broken all British records with his successes at Aintree and Cheltenham, while occasionally landing some of the bigger prizes on the flat. Two great flat racers, Ballymoss and Gladness, brought him international recognition and virtually forced him to go for the flat exclusively. Within a few years he had that side of the racing game at his feet as well. It was O'Brien who saw the potential of the great Canadian stallion, Northern Dancer, and he and his syndicate partners, son-in-law, John Magnier, and British businessman, Robert Sangster, had struck gold with this equine jewel's progeny before the rest of the racing world got the message. In recent times competition from Arabian racing interests has curtailed O'Brien's assaults on the international market, but he and his partners already own some of the most valuable stallions and mares in the world. It can be only a matter of time before the O'Brien syndicate breeds a champion of its own.

The O'Brien wizardry has been passed on to his son, David, who a few years ago trained Secreto to beat his father's El Gran Senor by a short head in the Epsom Derby. That brilliance and depth of experience will never be for sale and will remain Ireland's most valuable sporting asset.

ABOVE *Although the Olympic ideal means that sport is about taking part rather than winning, the competitive streak in the Irish has meant that the prize is eagerly competed for. At the end of the day however, both winner and loser can admire the trophy over a glass or two of Guinness.*

In a horse-mad country like Ireland, there are many other heroes, like the jockeys, Jonjo O'Neill, Pat Taaffe and Pat Eddery, but it is the great horses – Arkle, Prince Regent, Dawn Run and Nijinsky – that the people really love to remember. Arkle, trained by Tom Dreaper and ridden by Pat Taaffe, was so superior to his contemporary steeplechasers in the 1960s that the authorities in Britain and Ireland were forced to re-draft the rules of handicapping for races in which he was entered – one set of weights if he ran, another if he did not. It is most unlikely that this will ever again happen in National Hunt racing.

Show jumping has its Irish folk hero in Longford-born Eddie Macken, a former world champion, and there is also great interest in point-to-point racing and three-day-eventing.

Hunting has always attracted people from abroad, and foreigners also come for the summer racing festivals at Tralee, Killarney, Listowel, Tramore and, biggest of them all, Galway.

Greyhound racing and coursing have been described as the poor man's equivalent of the sport of kings, but it is far from that nowadays, as feeding and training costs have spiralled and the British market has become more selective.

Coursing has encountered severe opposition on the grounds of cruelty and moves are afoot all over the world to have the sport banned. However, it remains extremely popular in rural Ireland and just a few years ago a dog called Master Myles attracted an attendance in the region of 10,000 from all over

Ireland when he ran in the town of Abbeyfeale in County Limerick. He was later sold for £30,000 and died while being exercised two weeks later.

A century earlier a dog called Master McGrath earned immortality for Ireland by winning England's coursing classic, the Waterloo Cup, three times in four years. His memory was honoured by the erection of a monument dedicated to him on the outskirts of the town of Dungarvan in County Waterford. Last year the monument was damaged by opponents of the sport, but it has since been restored.

Greyhound racing continues to attract big attendances at tracks around the country and buyers from the United States, Australia and Great Britain are always interested in acquiring a top-class Irish dog. Spanish Battleship, winner of three Irish Derbys in succession, is safe in the record books, while in America they still speak of the feats of the great Rocking Ship, which was bred in Kerry, just as Master Myles and Spanish Battleship were.

Next to Gaelic games, rugby and soccer enjoy the most popularity among field sports in Ireland. Rugby tends to be supported by the well-to-do; soccer is strongest in working-class urban districts. There are colleges like Blackrock, Castleknock, Clongowes Wood and Belvedere in the Dublin area which concentrate on rugby as their specialist field game and produce many of Ireland's senior international players. At Limerick, somewhat exceptionally, rugby is the working man's game, and it was in that city that Munster beat the touring All-Blacks and thus became the first Irish side to beat a touring XV from world-dominating New Zealand.

In international competition success comes only spasmodically to Ireland, although almost every year the international side manages to produce a surprise victory over England, Wales or Scotland. Victory over France, especially in Paris, is rare. Yet Ireland has produced many world-class players, including Jack Kyle, Mike Gibson, Ollie Campbell, Fergus Slattery, Willie John McBride and Ken Goodall.

At one time a good rugby player was virtually guaranteed a successful business career, and Ireland's best-known international businessman, Dr. A. J. F. O'Reilly, the boss of the Heinz operation in Philadelphia, had an exclusively rugby background, having come from Belvedere through the Leinster, Irish, and Great Britain and Ireland Lions teams.

The Irish international rugby team is a 32-county selection, as distinct from soccer (for which the Republic of Ireland and Northern Ireland have separate teams), but it is doubtful if

rugby has been much of a unifying force in the Six Counties since few, if any, of the Roman Catholic community in the north play rugby. There is, however, considerable inter-club activity between clubs north and south of the border and the Republic's national anthem is played before international games in the Republic. Ireland no longer plays international rugby games north of the border.

Soccer is equally popular among both the Protestant and Roman Catholic communities in the north and rivalry between clubs of the different denominations is bitter and intense. Players from all clubs regularly play for Northern Ireland. Invariably, the best young players, north and south, are snapped up by scouts for British clubs and play their professional football in Great Britain. Nowadays regulations regarding eligibility to play international soccer are so loose that even having an Irish grandparent can qualify a player to play for Ireland, and there are amusing stories of foreign-born players not recognizing the strains of the Irish national anthem when it is played before their international debut. The Republic of Ireland side is comprised entirely of foreign-based players and in 1986 the former England World Cup star, Jack Charlton, who hasn't a drop of Irish blood in him, was appointed team manager.

Despite its lack of international success in soccer the country has produced some of the best players ever seen in Europe, including George Best, Jackie Carey and Pat Jennings. Best, it was generally admitted, had the talent to win a place on any World XI, but his penchant for falling foul of authority and for making the wrong kind of headlines through his spectacular lifestyle put an untimely end to his career. He attempted several comebacks and played in the United States for a while, but he never looked like recapturing his former brilliance.

Best has a kindred spirit in his fellow-Belfastman, Alex Higgins, the man who more than anybody else earned snooker the phenomenal popularity it enjoys around the world today. Higgins tried to become a jockey before he took up snooker seriously, but he found the discipline of racing too demanding and saw snooker as a much more attractive alternative. He arrived on the snooker scene just as television was looking for a winter sport to enliven the long evenings (and sell colour television sets) and his tearaway style, which earned him the name 'Hurricane', was an instant hit with the viewers. He won the world championship in 1972 and 1982, but he has attracted damaging publicity far too often, and although he retains his magnetism for some viewers, he can no longer assert that snooker cannot do without him.

Ireland's other world snooker champion, Denis Taylor, of Tyrone, is a different type of man. Exemplary in his private life and a great wit when he plays the exhibition circuit, Taylor gave one of the best performances in snooker history when he came from eight frames behind with nine to play and beat the reigning champion, Steve Davis, on the last ball in the 1985 world championship final.

Not surprisingly, Ireland, with its glorious scenery and splendid seaside locations, has some first-class golf courses and quite a few top players. Tom Watson, the American legend, has rated Ballybunion, in County Kerry, as one of his favourite links courses in the world; just a few miles away, at Barrow, near Tralee, is the course designed by Arnold Palmer as his European showpiece. Killarney has two splendid courses, Waterville is a tigerish test, Portmarnock and Royal Dublin are world famous, and Portrush, Lahinch, Rosses Point and County Louth's Baltray attract thousands of visitors from all over the globe each year.

Christy O'Connor, Harry Bradshaw, Fred Daly, Joe Carr, Norman Drew, Philomena Garvey, Clarrie Reddan, Mary McKenna and Claire Hourihane made world headlines and when Europe beat the United States in Ohio to retain the Ryder Cup in 1987, it was appropriate that another Irishman, Eamonn Darcy, should have played a crucial role.

Although not everybody uses the phrase, the 'Fighting Irish', as a compliment, Ireland has made a wonderful contribution to boxing history. John L. Sullivan claimed to be Irish and at one time nearly every hungry fighter who made good in America seemed to have Irish blood in his veins. Certainly there was no disputing the Irishness of the great Jimmy McLarnin, who took part in some of the greatest welterweight and middleweight championship battles in ring history. Rinty Monaghan won a world flyweight title and used to delight the fans with his post-fight renderings of 'When Irish Eyes Are Smiling'; more recently Barry McGuigan, of Clones in County Monaghan, brought the country to its feet with a series of battling victories that culminated in his winning the world featherweight title in Belfast. Jack Doyle, the Cork-born Irish Guardsman, was another fighting singer, or singing fighter, though after a disastrous visit to the United States in the 1930s it was conceded that he sang like Dempsey and boxed like McCormack.

Many other sports – basketball, hockey, cricket, sailing, swimming, indeed virtually every sport that does not require snow or ice – is thriving in Ireland. The Irish love their sport and they idolise their sportsmen. Ask Stephen Roche!

'THE FIGHTING IRISH' •

Jack Dempsey, 'The Manassa Mauler' was born in Manassa, Colorado on June 24 1895. He is one of the long line of successful Irish-American sportsmen – not just boxers, but baseball players like Michael Kelly, whose base-running was immortalized in the song 'Slide, Kelly, Slide', and football players and coaches like John Joseph McGraw who led the New York Giants to ten championships. The Irish have taken their love of sport all over the world; in recent years Jim Stynes, born in Dublin, played Gaelic football for the city and then emigrated to Australia. Both he and Sean Wight, a Kerry footballer, now play Australian rules, and both returned to play against Ireland in the 1987 Ireland-Australia match. Dempsey won the world heavyweight title on July 4 1919, beating Jess Willard. The 6 ft 6 in Willard was an incredible 70 pounds heavier than the challenger, and firm favourite. Dempsey knocked him down seven times in the first round, broke his jaw and ribs, and took the crown in the third. The savagery of his early attack may be explained by the rumour that he bet his whole purse, at odds of ten to one, that he would knock out the champion in the first round – thus living up to two clichéd images of the Irishman – as fighter and gambler. Dempsey won against the French world light-heavyweight champion Carpentier by a knock-out in the fourth round. This fight took the first million-dollar gate in boxing history.

RIGHT *The Irish-American John Lawrence Sullivan became world heavyweight champion in 1883, and in doing so established boxing as a respectable and highly popular sport for the first time. Statuettes like this one were sold for five dollars each to commemorate the victory. The first world heavyweight title fight with gloves and three-minute rounds was between Sullivan and 'Gentleman' John Corbett on 7 September 1892, in New Orleans. Corbett won in 21 rounds.*

LEFT *Barry McGuigan won the world featherweight title on 8 June 1985, against Eusabio Pedrosa, in Belfast, McGuigan's success brought together the Catholic and Protestant communities for a few moments of glorious celebration. When he fought in London, Catholics and Protestants travelled together across the water to cheer him on. McGuigan was aware of this almost accidental power for reconciliation which he represented, and he stepped into the ring with the dove of peace emblazoned on his robe.*

INTERNATIONAL HEAVYWEIGH CHAMPIONSHIP OF THE WORLD

Jack Dempsey VS Georges Carpentier

THIRTY ACRES OVAL JERSEY CITY N.J.
JULY 2, 1921
UNDER TH___ANAGEMENT OF ___ RICKARD

Preliminary Bouts to World's Heavyweight Championship
Saturday, July 2, 1921

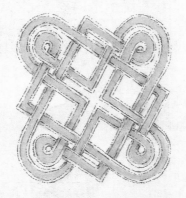

BELFAST
AND ITS
TROUBLES

The city is built on mud and wrath
Its weather is predicted; its street lamps
Light up in the glowering, crowded evenings.
Time switches, ripped from them are clamped
To sticks of sweet, sweating explosive
All the machinery of a state
Is a set of scales that squeezes out blood.

TOM PAULIN
A STATE OF JUSTICE

148

A traveller in Ireland, visiting the city of Belfast for the first time, may well be struck by the contrast it provides with the rest of the country. The city may be historically divided between Orange and Green, but the colour which permeates most of the area is the more neutral one of grey. Belfast was the only Irish city which really undertook an industrial revolution in the 19th century and the city is dominated by the symbols of that experience. The image is greatly strengthened by the fact that most of the industrial centres on which the Victorian wealth of the city were based are now crumbling, hollow wrecks, scars on a landscape like those in so many of the inner-city areas of Great Britain. Yes, that is what really differentiates this grey and foreboding city from much of the rest of Ireland. Belfast has an undeniably British feel about it. Whereas everything about Dublin, Galway and Cork is Irish, Belfast is the one city where the imperial influence is visibly dominant. On the face of it, it appears to have far more in common with the declining inner cities of England, such as Liverpool, Sheffield and Birmingham, than with any Irish equivalents. That, however, is only on the face of it, and to observe the north of Ireland in such a way is misleading.

In many ways Belfast may be atypical, but it does contain within its great sprawling mass of buildings and people most of the contradictions and complexities which make the six counties of Ulster that still remain in the United Kingdom such a confusing, violent, fascinating and frightening place. Within Belfast's boundaries live approximately 400,000 of the 1.5 million people of the north. Here 'the troubles', as they are blandly called, are at their most concentrated. The proximity of rival areas, peoples and factions is far greater here, the problems are more explicit, more brutal and more naked. If, as an outsider, you manage to understand the driving forces behind the conflict in Belfast, then you have gone a long way towards understanding the nature of the long, tragic, and seemingly never-ending saga of Anglo-Irish relations and their debilitating effects on the lives of ordinary men and women.

Central to the lives of Belfast's inhabitants is the constant interplay of normality and abnormality. The city centre may appear like any other thriving metropolis. On a typical Saturday morning the shops are full and the scene could be any busy city centre. Closer examination, however, reveals that there are armed soldiers on the street and security gates on the entrance to the pedestrianized shopping centre. No cars are allowed into

the centre, not to stop traffic congestion but as a safeguard against car bombs. Entering any shop may involve being searched by a security guard. You can never quite forget that Belfast is not just another city.

Dominating the centre is Belfast's impressive city hall, a fine building with the hallmarks of Great Britain's imperial past stamped all over it. Opened in 1906 after eight years of building, it is the meeting place of the city council. The interior is an utter delight, especially the marvellous marbled staircase and the elaborate artwork on the fine dome of the building.

Close by is the far less impressive Europa hotel. In modern

to the Divis flats. It is difficult to believe that this impersonal construction, which exudes alienation from every one of its many cracks, boarded windows and patches of damp, was built only in 1968. By the end of the 1970s it was a haven for violence, drugs and disease, a living monument to the planners and architects who never had to live in such places.

The Divis complex backs on to the area known as the Falls, the name of which has become synonymous with the power and significance of the rebel Republican movement. Since 1983 this area has been represented in the British House of Commons by Gerry Adams of Sinn Fein, the party committed to the removal of the British presence from Ireland, by force if necessary. The Falls exudes the atmosphere of a war zone and it is hard to believe that it is only 15 minutes from the city centre. The army drives through the area at high speed, seemingly feeling at risk to do otherwise. There is the sight of charred, boarded-up buildings, legacies of either popular uprising or terrorist madness, depending on which explanation you wish to listen to. Violence has dominated this area for the last 20 years – the most recent expression of militancy in an area which has often appeared to be part of the United Kingdom in name only. The most striking evidence of political opposition is the huge number of ornate wall murals. These eulogize the Republican dead, trying to convince the passer-by that a Republican who died in 1916 was fighting for the same cause as those who have died in the 1980s. The most numerous images on the walls recall the summer of 1981, when 10 Republican prisoners, some of them local men, starved themselves to death in a British prison, demanding that they be treated not as common criminals but as prisoners of war.

The people of the Falls have lived within this embattled zone for so long now and the consequences are there for all to see. There are children who have known nothing but violence. They shout abuse at the passing military personnel with a lack of fear which comes from knowing little else. The old women gossip on the front door porches, probably wondering whether they will ever see a new dawn. The men make idle conversation on street corners; few have anything better to do in an area where 80 per cent of men are out of work.

There is a vast number of black taxi cabs in the area. The Falls Road taxi cabs are unlike their counterparts in London's West End. There are no restrictions on the number of passengers and many of the cabs appear to be bursting at the seams. The taxi man has passed into local folklore; a local song has sprung from nowhere about this phenomenon.

ABOVE *British soldiers on the streets of Ireland, just outside Belfast. For the locals this is now part of everyday life; the army has been in Northern Ireland since 1969.*

times the hotel has been the centre for those people who travel to Belfast to report on the Troubles. The clinking of glasses in the bar as the journalists share gossip and half-truths has become the hallmark of the most bombed building in Belfast. Next door to the Europa is one of the city's cultural centres, the Opera House. Its reopening in the 1980s symbolized a partial return to normality.

If the overall atmosphere of the centre is that of a city in which normality and abnormality compete for prominence, there is no doubt which is the victor just a few short minutes away. Turning down the Grosvenor Road you eventually come

THIS PAGE AND RIGHT *Loyalist murals are to be found in many Protestant working class areas. They celebrate the victory of Protestantism in 17th century Ireland, and the pride of the community in being part of Britain.*

LEFT *The Troubles are not confined to Belfast of course; ugly clashes involving the police and civil rights marchers in Londonderry, in October and November 1968, were an important spur to the arrival of British troops.*

ABOVE LEFT *The Easter rising of 1916 was an unsuccessful attempt by Irish Republicans to seize power. The legacy of the rising still reverberates around Ireland today.*

ABOVE *Mural on the wall of the Sinn Fein offices on the Falls Road in Belfast. The murals are a major symbol of resistance to British rule. This particular mural has been destroyed by a petrol bomb. The rocks are there to prevent the parking of cars, which may be boobytrapped.*

LEFT *A major source of the present Troubles was the awful distress on the land in the 19th century.*

As I roamed out through Belfast town around by Castle Street,
A-seeking transportation a young man I did meet.
They said his name was Cosgrove,
Some called him Desperate Dan,
For he risked his life ten times a day
As a Falls Road taxi man.
Well I put two bob into his hand,
I climbed into the car,
Well that was all they charged us for travelling near and far.
With fourteen other passengers we made a noble band,
As we set out from Sawyers with the Falls Road taxi man.

ABOVE *One of the symbols of British rule in Northern Ireland are the law courts in Belfast. Heavily fortified, it is here that* *many of the trials involving paramilitaries have taken place.*

These cabs date from the early 1970s, when other forms of public transport ceased to travel down the road. They are now the main source of travel between the Falls and the city centre.

The Falls is but a few minutes from the city centre: more intriguing is the proximity of this Republican stronghold to the heartland of Protestant Belfast, the Shankill Road. At first glance one could be excused for believing that the peoples of the two areas are the same. They are the same colour, they dress the same and they both appear to live in the same, run-down inner-city housing. The differences, however, are vast.

The sectarian allegiances of the working-class communities of Belfast are legendary. Michael McLaverty observed this phenomenon many years ago, in *Call My Brother Back*, but little has changed. 'Supposin' ye got all the Orange sashes and all the green sashes in this town and ye tied them round loaves of bread and flung them over Queen's bridge, what would happen? ... The gulls – the gulls that fly in the air, what would they do? They'd go for the bread! But you – the other gulls – would go for the sashes every time.'

For outsiders the state of conflict between the ordinary people of Northern Ireland is mystifying, but when sectarianism

154

is grounded in nationality and religion, it is a mould that is desperately difficult to break. The Falls people have an allegiance to a united Ireland and some of them are prepared to use paramilitary means to achieve this goal. The Shankill is just as committed to staying out of any united Irish framework and remaining part of the United Kingdom. The Falls produces volunteers for the provisional IRA; the Shankill has its own groups, such as the Ulster Defence Association and the Ulster Volunteer Force. The tragedy is that in nearly all respects the communities share the same problems – bad housing and unemployment are the most pressing – but their deep and bitter division is symbolized by a high 'peace' wall, keeping the two peoples apart.

The Shankill has changed beyond all recognition in the last 15 years, devastated by the separate efforts of the planners and the bombers. Proud, neat, terraced houses with highly polished front porches have been replaced by impersonal, purpose-built blocks. The effect has been to destroy community values and foster anonymity.

There is almost as much graffitti here as in the Falls. There are references to King Billy and 1690, to the Boyne and the Red Hand of Ulster, to Queen Elizabeth II and the Union of Great Britain and Northern Ireland. All of these commemorate the victory of Protestantism over Roman Catholicism in the 17th century and of Unionism over nationalism in the 20th.

One of the influences on the decision by the Protestant working classes in the last century to oppose Home Rule was the economic strength of the city, the industrial base of which so differentiated Belfast from the rest of Ireland. As one speaker against Home Rule argued at the turn of the century, 'Belfast has done very well under the union: her population has quadrupled in 50 years and her wage rates are higher than anywhere else in Ireland and in some cases up to British standards.'

At the heart of that industrial prosperity were the shipyards of Harland and Wolff. Still towering over east Belfast are the huge booms of this legendary workplace, which symbolized the economic benefits of staying British rather than being sucked into an agrarian Republic. At their height these shipyards employed some 26,000 workers, nearly all of them Protestant and Unionist. Today only 5,000 are employed, victims of cheaper foreign competition and a drop in demand for shipping throughout the modern world. The affluence of many Protestant workers has greatly diminished and unemployment is a common feature in the Protestant heartlands, a fact that would have been unthinkable only a few short years ago.

ABOVE *The Red Hand of Ulster, a symbol of loyalism engraved in glass.*

RIGHT *The IRA parade their colours in 1985, an open display of their resistance to the British presence. Colour parties like these are now very rare.*

Travelling eastwards out of the urban squalor of the city centre, the visitor is surrounded by far less cluttered suburbs. Eventually he arrives at the parliament building at Stormont, opened in 1932 by the Prince of Wales, later Edward VIII. The sheer size of the building and its long, regimented drive are instantly striking. The front is dominated by a large statue of Edward Carson, the intrepid spokesman who led the Ulster Unionists to partition in 1921. He gestures towards the city, which lies below the hills on which the parliament building stands. It is difficult to believe that this building housed the parliament for a territory of a mere million and a half people. Its grandeur was, as much as anything, a celebration of the defeat of Irish nationalism in Ulster.

The grand old building is no longer in use, since Northern Ireland no longer has a devolved parliament. The term 'Stormont' has come to be synonymous with a period in history, from 1921 to 1972, when Ulster Unionist governments were allowed to exercise unbridled power in the north.

Belfast has undergone significant changes in recent years, especially in the south side of the city. This district, based on the Malone Road and Stranmillis area, has long been associated with the affluent middle classes. There are large Georgian houses, inhabited by academics and lawyers. The impressive growth of restaurants and evening entertainment spots provide yet another example of the juxtaposition between normality and abnormality in the city. Here, just a couple of miles from the Falls and the Shankill, it is difficult to remember that you are in a battle-torn city.

The University dominates the south side of the city. Built at the turn of the century, it has long been the one institution in which participation is not dependent on which foot you kick with (Catholics are often referred to as left-footers). It has rightly won a reputation as one of the most prestigious seats of learning in the United Kingdom.

For all its problems, all its conflicts and all its bitterness, Belfast retains an essential goodness, as visitors to the city well know. The kindness to strangers is not false. It is the product of a kind-hearted people who are caught up in a conflict that is bigger than any of them. Perhaps the final word should be left to an Irish outsider, Micheál MacLiammóir, who summed up his ambiguous attitude to the city in 1949. 'Impossible to fathom why I like the city but I do. Admittedly a cold sort of place even in the radiant northern April ... but there is something about it all, its fantastic practicability, its bleak, bowler-hatted refusal of the inevitable!'

ABOVE *Harland and Wolff shipyard: an overwhelmingly Protestant workforce, the employment of whose very skills was an expression of support for British imperialism worldwide.*

RIGHT *The IRA address a rally in 1974; in that year, attempts by Westminster to establish a Council of Ireland led to a Protestant general strike.*

OPPOSITE *Stormont Castle, the seat of the ill-fated Northern Ireland Assembly. When Captain Terence O'Neill became Prime Minister in 1963, his policy of reconciliation at home and with the south led to dangerous fears among the Protestant majority and more strident demands for real change from the Catholic communities. The escalation of violence had led to the arrival of British troops by 1969, and in 1972 the Northern Ireland Constitution was suspended and direct rule instituted from Westminster through a secretary of state.*

• STORMONT CASTLE •

THE IRISH ABROAD

The Kennedy Memorial Park in New Ross,
County Wexford, home of President John F
Kennedy's ancestors.

 Islands are often more crossroads than starting points, and the island of Ireland is no exception. Foreigners have been arriving in Ireland since time immemorial and the Irish have been leaving and settling abroad since records began. The 'Irish abroad' comprise a vast and amorphous throng of great diversity. It includes those fresh from Ireland and those who feel Irish only on St Patrick's Day; those whom the Irish nation claim because of an accident of birth, but who might not recognize themselves as Irish; and, of course, all those 'honorary' Irish from other countries who have contributed their efforts to Ireland and the Irish.

They came from every background and they could be found at every level of society in the places where they settled. Aristocrats, labourers, political refugees, transportees, comfortable farmers and smallholders, all took the boat. Many found security in their adopted countries; a few rose to positions of power and luxury or lived to see their children do so. Half a dozen United States presidents, a couple of British prime ministers, a French premier, an Argentinian dictator and a Chilean liberator, even a rajah (from Tipperary) – all claim Irish background or ancestry.

We know a great deal about the successful because their careers have made them famous. But the history of the mass of migrants is more elusive. Many, for one reason or another, disguised their origins; many were assimilated by their adopted cultures; others emigrated before proper records began. Many from Ulster defined themselves as 'Scotch-Irish' and created a national identity of their own. In this way sections of the Irish population 'disappeared' from history.

Nevertheless, there is much that we do know about the Irish even before the age of statistics or the printed word. Two separate migratory impulses scattered Irish names across the continent. The first was religion, which created little colonies of monks and scholars abroad for some four centuries after the fall of the Roman empire. They established churches and settlements in some 40 European cities, stretching from Kiev in Russia to Lucca in Italy and north to Iona in Scotland. Sometimes they worked as missionaries; in lands already Christian they saw themselves as reformers and teachers, bringing erring Christian communities back into the Roman fold. They do not easily fit into the category of emigrants, for they were neither induced to go by the promise of better things abroad nor driven by tyranny or deprivation at home. Instead, as followers of the

• QUEENSTOWN, LIVERPOOL, NEW YORK •

dictum of God to Abraham in the Old Testament, 'Go forth from thy country, from thy kin and thy family, to the country that I shall show thee', they turned from solitude of their Irish hermitages towards a new and foreign isolation. Their dedication was to Rome rather than Ireland, however they initiated the romantic conception of Irish settlement and achievement abroad and gained for Ireland a reputation as a land of saints and scholars.

War and war's disruption provided the stimulus for the second wave of migrants in the 16th century, when Elizabeth I and the Stuart monarchs defeated the chiefs of Gaelic and Anglo-Norman Ireland. A series of brutal military campaigns transformed the fragmented world of Medieval Ireland. The old aristocracy and its followers were forced into exile and replaced by a new commercial elite. Pasture was replaced by arable farming, communal and tribal land by rented farms. The result was population growth and the concentration of wealth in the hands of an ostentatious, but insecure, Protestant 'Ascendancy'. Historians estimate that from the 'Flight of the Earls' in 1607 to the end of the 18th century some 400,000 Irish soldiers and their women left Ireland to fight for European powers. They sought alliances with Catholic states sympathetic to the Stuart cause in the hope of ousting the Protestant conquerors from Great Britain. They enjoyed an exalted position in European courts and were showered with honours and wealth beyond anything they had known in Ireland. The rewards of the foot soldier were more modest – adventure, fairly regular pay and, in the event of his death, pensions for his widow and orphans. The Irish were not, of course, unique as soldiers fighting for foreign causes. They were one of the many peoples from peripheral or mountainous areas – Picardy, Corsica, Sardinia, Wales and, most notably, Switzerland – that provided the great tide of mercenaries who helped the French and Spanish monarchies to reshape the map of Europe according to their imperial designs.

In peacetime many of those Irish soldiers formed little colonies in Dutch, French and Spanish towns and from them emerged a network of merchants engaged in the developing colonial trade. From Rotterdam down the Atlantic coast as far as Cadiz there were Irish merchant houses. Some cities, like Bordeaux, had as many as 20 such establishments, nearly all of them controlled by Roman Catholic families from the counties of Limeric and Galway. They issued bills of exchange, provided credit and generally assisted trade between Dublin, London, the continent and the New World.

LEFT *A ragged, caricatured Irishman considers emigrating to America in this lithograph from 1854. Cheap fares contributed to increased immigration, though for many the journey was a hell of seasickness, disease (including typhoid and cholera) and terrible overcrowding.*

RIGHT *Born in Ireland and brought to America as a child in 1815, Mike Walsh became one of the first political spokesmen for Irish immigrants. He was elected to Congress in 1850, where he served until his death in 1859.*

MIKE WALSH.

The People's Champion

Links between the New World and the Old were reinforced by the establishment of Irish settlers in the West Indies. From all over the British Isles impoverished and landless victims of war were transported in large numbers to the Caribbean. Besides those who were compelled to go, others with money bought cheap land and settled there, as well as in the new colony of Virginia. Tales of success made their way across the ocean to people who had little to hope for in Ireland and many a penniless man sold himself as an indentured labourer in exchange for a ship's passage across the Atlantic. Irish merchants, entrepreneurs and the Roman Catholic gentry, deprived of their status by the operation of the penal laws, bought land and ran sugar plantations in the West Indies. Several islands, Montserrat and Antigua in particular, were dominated by Irish planters. With the abolition of the slave trade in the early 19th century the Irish connection withered, leaving only a few colonies of poor men and women behind. They became known as the 'Black Irish'.

Outside the Atlantic world there were also Irish connections with India. Rivalry between the European powers in India frequently involved Irish troops. Thomas, Lally, from County Galway, led an Irish brigade in the service of France and won a

162

BELOW *The annual St Patrick's Day parade in New York is a chance for the Irish to display pride in their cultural heritage.*

series of engagements before being stopped at the battle of Wandiwash by the British under the command of Eyre Coote – another Irishman (for County Limerick). Although Irish commercial links with India were few – a matter of grievance to 18th-century patriots – a number of individuals, like Laurence Sullivan, played influential parts in the operations of the East India Company. Perhaps the most remarkable of these was George Thompson, a poor labourer from County Tipperary, who went to sea in his youth and managed by a mixture of luck and military ability to carve out the Sikh state of Hariana in northern India which he ruled in splendour for many years.

London, as the centre of empire, had Irish banking connections. The Fitzgeralds, Kirwans, Lynches, Husseys, Burkes and Tuites were among the most important Irish banking families and most had premises and businesses in the Moorfields district of London. During the Gordon Riots of 1780, the last serious outburst of anti-Catholic violence in the capital, nearly all suffered damage at the hands of Protestant mobs.

London was also a cultural centre for Irish poets, actors and playrights. The wealth and population of the capital meant more readers and theatre-goers, more patrons and more critics, all of which attracted Irish writers to seek fame in England. Congreve, Farquhar, Steele, Sheridan and Goldsmith need no introduction, but there were dozens of lesser figures. How many today have heard of Thomas Southerne, who wrote the first play denouncing the slave trade, or Charles Coffey, who introduced traditional Irish music into London stage plays? It is true that most of these early writers were descendents of English settlers in Ireland, but traditional Gaelic names appear with increasing frequency – Arthur Murphy, Hugh Kelly, John O'Keefe, Patrick Delaney and many more.

Irish writers contributed to doctrines of colonial nationalism which developed in both Ireland and America. Swift, Lucas, Molyneaux and Grattan developed these arguments in Ireland; Edmund Burke and Lord Shelbourne did so in London; and Francis Alison, Charles Thomson, Thomas McKean, George Read and others brought them to fruition in the American

RIGHT *Wealthy Irish Americans organized fundraising social events to aid the Irish poor. In the late 19th century, funds from the United States were not merely a gesture, but contributed significantly to a better standard of living for those at home.*

colonies in 1776. This last group was part of the large Ulster Presbytarian influx into America which occurred at this time. This was mainly a migration of men and the absence of Ulster women in the colonies may explain the rapid integration of the Irish into the American population, as they married into the local community. Poor harvests, low linen prices and religious oppression prompted the emigration and encouraged political opinions supporting American independence from Great Britain. Five of the signatories of the Declaration of Independence, its printer, and the secretary of the Congress that adopted it, were of Irish background.

The French Revolution brought a change in emigration patterns. Revolutionary France was unsympathetic to Catholic emigrés such as the 'Wild Geese'. America, on the other hand, was eager for more settlers and offered an attractive alternative. Great Britain, too, was experiencing a revolution of sorts, and industrial development offered a chance of employment to the Irish poor, whose numbers had multiplied many times during the previous decades.

The new steamship services between Ireland and Great Britain in the 1820s opened up England and Scotland to seasonal labourers. The sea journey could be made for as little as sixpence and some migrants were carried free across the Irish Sea as ballast by returning Welsh coal boats from Leinster. Once landed, they travelled in families to the main agricultural districts of Great Britain, attending hiring fairs in Scotland, particularly those in Forfar, Renfrew and Lanarkshire, and moving southwards over the border to meet other parties of Irish in the agricultural districts of Lincolnshire and Kent. At the end of each season most of them made their way back to Ireland with their savings; but a number of them stayed on in the new industrial villages that were developing round the water-powered textile industries of Lancashire and Yorkshire. London, too, provided permanent homes for people who saw no point in returning to their tiny plots. The Wapping dockland area, the Marylebone gravel pits and the Seven Dials district (now Covent Garden) were the main settlement areas of Irish poor in the capital, and many continued to take seasonal agricultural employment, such as hop-picking in Kent, long after establishing themselves as city-dwellers.

The advent of steampower transformed the towns into cities attracting still more migrants. In the first half of the 19th century the largest Irish colonies were in Liverpool, Dundee and Glasgow, followed by Manchester, Birmingham, Leeds and Bradford. The Irish concentrated in areas of cheap, unsanitary housing, which came to be known by such names as 'Irishtown' or 'Little Ireland'. Practices common in the Irish countryside – faction-fighting, the keeping of animals in close proximity to, or within, human habitations and long wakes which delayed the burial of the dead – presented hazards in an urban setting, whether the city was Belfast, Birmingham or Boston. Many of these practices were already ending in Ireland itself.

In this hostile and poverty-striken world the Irish immigrant often turned to political radicalism, a radicalism which had roots in the agrarian struggle at home in the late 18th century. Men like Bronterre O'Brien and Feargus O'Connor led the Chartist demands for parliamentary reform in the 1830s and 1840s. John Doherty made the first attempt to create a unified trade union organisation as a counterbalance to the power of employers. A highly politicised people, the Irish quickly adjusted to the realities of industrial politics. Once dedicated to a cause they proved tough adversaries, as the superintendent of the Manchester Watch testified: 'In order to apprehend on Irishman in the Irish parts of town, we are forced to take ten or

ABOVE *Many Irishmen arriving in the United States in the 1840s and 1850s and elsewhere (including England) were employed as labourers. Cartoons like this one (1882) prove that the caricature of the Irish 'navvy' was a hard one to shake off. They also of course ignore the fact that without such immigrant labour, even as recently as in the 1960s, Britain would have no motorway network. A New York newspaper understood this a century earlier:*
'America demands for her development an inexhaustible fund of physical energy . . . waterpower, steam-power, and Irish-power. The last works hardest of all.'

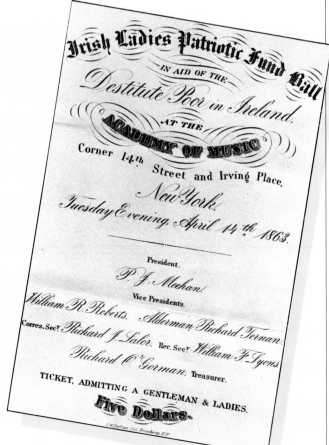

Irish Ladies Patriotic Fund Ball

IN AID OF THE

Destitute Poor in Ireland.

AT THE

ACADEMY OF MUSIC

Corner 14th Street and Irving Place,

New York,

Tuesday Evening April 14th 1863.

President.
P. J. Meehan.

Vice Presidents.
William R. Roberts. Alderman Richard Ternan.

Corres. Sec'y Richard J. Lalor. Rec. Sec'y William F. Lyons.

Richard O'Gorman. Treasurer.

TICKET, ADMITTING A GENTLEMAN & LADIES.

Five Dollars.

164

• THE KENNEDYS •

F D Roosevelt appointed self-
made millionaire businessman
Joseph P Kennedy Chairman of the
Securities and Exchange
Commission, then of the Maritime
Commission, and finally
Ambassador to Great Britain. The
1930s Depression-inspired anti-
Republican backlash saw many
newly elected Irish-American
Democratic senators and
congressmen on their way to
Washington. It was then that the
foundations of Joseph's ambitions
for his sons were laid. John
Fitzgerald, with his father's money
and influence on the big-city
Democratic machinery behind him,
hardly put a foot wrong on the
road to the Whitehouse: a
decorated naval hero at 29, he was
elected to the House of
Representatives in 1946 and to the
Senate in 1952. In 1961 he became
the first Catholic president; his
assassination was in 1963. Five years
later his brother Senator Robert F
Kennedy met the same fate after
becoming a presidential candidate.
Only the youngest brother,
Edward, remains, the Massachusetts
Senator. John F Kennedy's
administration had consistently
supported liberal Democratic
principles following the shameful
McCarthy era, and his death is seen
by many as a great tragedy in
American 20th-century political life.

FAR LEFT *President John F Kennedy at a press conference in 1963.*

BELOW LEFT *As President-elect, JFK shakes hands with Father Richard J Casey, pastor of Holy Trinity Catholic Church in Washington DC. Kennedy was inaugurated that afternoon.*

LEFT, AND BELOW *The ancestral home of the original Kennedys in New Ross, County Wexford.*

RIGHT *The 'Kennedy compound', Joseph P Kennedy's summer home in Hyannisport, Cape Cod, purchased in 1926; this house, and the houses of John and Robert on the same site, have become a major tourist attraction, such is the mystique of the Kennedy dynasty.*

BELOW RIGHT *The Kennedy Memorial Park in County Wexford; when JFK was assassinated in 1963, the whole world mourned. The loss was perhaps more keenly felt in Ireland, to see a great man of Irish stock and the first Catholic president cut down.*

twenty, or even more, watchmen.'

Of course, not all the Irish were labour radicals. 'Orange' violence from time to time threatened Catholic Irish communities. Glasgow and Liverpool were both cities where religious animosity sharpened the struggle between native and migrant workers. The 1851 Murphy riots, led by the Protestant Irish demagogue, William Murphy, demonstrated that Irish divisions could be imported into the immigrant communities.

Middle-class opinion often expressed contempt for the labouring population and the Irish at the bottom of the heap became the butt of humour and abuse. Political cartoonists on both sides of the Atlantic portrayed aspects of Irish life unflatteringly. Sir John Tenniel drew the nationalist supporters of Daniel O'Connell and, later, the Fenians who placed bombs in London as simian morons, while the American Thomas Nast's bugbear was the Roman Catholic clergy, whom he depicted leading an inane-looking Irish flock. The political questions behind these images raised powerful emotive responses, not only among the Americans and British, but, in a profoundly divisive way, from the Irish themselves. There were many Irish Catholics who agreed with Bishop Moriarty's sentiment about 'hell not being hot enough' for Fenians; and Fenians like John Mitchel sneered at O'Connell as 'Poor old Dan, wonderful, mighty, jovial . . . smile of treachery, heart of unfathomable fraud'. With antagonisms like these among the Irish it is perhaps not surprising that the Irish cartoonist, Richard Doyle, who worked for *Punch*, saw nothing anti-Irish in Tenniel's work, but resigned

QUEENSTOWN

over an attack on the papacy in 1850.

The great Famine of 1847 shook the already crumbling structure of Irish society and caused an enormous exodus of land-hungry peasants. Even those people who had been regarded as comfortable farmers sunk now, overburdened by poor rates, into poverty themselves. During the course of the disaster and the following decades well over a million people fled from Ireland. Starving, sickly and wretched, they left by whatever means they could for the cities of Great Britain, Canada and the United States. Neither transportation nor cities could cope with this tide of human misery. Liverpool – the first step for many on the journey to America – presented scenes of turmoil and tragedy in the years 1847 to 1850. Lodging-house owners, ships' captains, American employers' agents, loan sharks and charlatans all touted for trade among the dispossessed who were desperate to escape from famine.

For those people who were lucky enough to survive the overcrowded conditions, the sea-sickness and the fever that overcame many during the passage, things were little better in America. New York, the main point of disembarkation, teemed with migrants, struggling in sweat shops to pay off debts or to find money to finance their journey further south or west to the frontier. Few took advantage of homesteading; having left Irish farms, they had little desire to start others in America.

During the 1850s conditions were harsh for the great mass of poor, Irish-speaking migrants. During the Civil War, however, they managed to carve out a social and political niche for themselves. Their role in battles like that of Fredericksburg, in which both the Confederate and Union camps depended on Irish regiments like the 'Fighting 69', boosted their status at a crucial time in America's history, allowing them to take advantage of the opening up of the West and bringing them social and economic security during the post-war boom decades before the next wave of migrants arrival from eastern and southern Europe. Nearly 20 per cent of the 2,865,028 men called into Federal service were recent immigrants, and the Irish Brigade were the most famous.

That was the period when fortunes were made. John Doheny made his from oil and James Flood from silver (he discovered the largest pocket in the world). Thomas Fortune Ryan (the middle name is apt, but in fact was derived from his maternal grandparents, who brought him up after he was orphaned at 14) gained his wealth from a variety of sources: railways, the New York Transit System, diamond mines, tobacco and life insurance. Joseph P Kennedy's successful specu-

BELOW RIGHT *President Ronald Reagan payed a visit to his ancestral home in Ballysporeen, County Tipperary, in 1984.*

lations on the stock exchange laid the foundation of a political dynasty. Peter McDonnell began as a penniless immigrant and graduated from there to become a stock-exchange millionaire. And Thomas E Murray, Edison's partner, made his money through a series of industrial inventions. Those are a few of the more spectacular examples; but even the more modest achievements were influential in suggesting to relatives back home that anyone could get rich in America. All over Europe, not just Ireland, these success stories cut the social ties that held inviduals to scraps of unproductive land. It was not simply eviction notices and transportation orders that kept the vast Atlantic traffic moving: the pull of success exercised a far stronger influence.

Canada, Australia and New Zealand also attracted thriving Irish settlements, though never on the American scale. Perhaps the isolation and emptiness of those distant lands weakened their attraction for a people who so loved community and conviviality. Those Irish who did make their homes in these unpeopled lands had cause to echo the words of Maurice O'Reilly in 1893:

We prize the men of the Southland so,
for the grasp of their kindly hand;
For a freedom as wide as the ocean's flow,
For the welcome with which they sought to show
That theirs was no foreign strand;
Till we almost acclaimed it 'home' – but, no,
It is not our own dear land.

The Irish in Great Britain, meanwhile, were consolidating their position. The establishment of a nationalist party at Westminster in the 1870s brought Ireland to the forefront of British politics. Irish MPs voiced Irish grievances in parliament and Irish journalists in London printed their comments for a large newspaper audience. Nationalism, Labour radicalism and the Catholic Church all had, to varying degrees, the support of the Irish in Great Britain. Two of the leaders of the 1889 dock strike for higher wages ('the dockers tanner'), Ben Tillett and James Twomey were of Irish extraction, as were a great number of the dockers. The strike had the support of Irish nationalist politicians and the dispute was finally settled by the intervention of Cardinal Manning.

Some identifiable Irish businesses were also established at this time, though none on the American scale. Michael Rochford, who came over in the 'hungry forties', started a large market-gardening business in Tottenham which is still going today. Thomas Lipton built up a retailing empire. Hugh McCalmont, from County Antrim, made millions on the London stock exchange.

Given the geographical proximity of Great Britain and Ireland and the political union of the two countries, few of those businessmen may have regarded themselves as 'migrants' in the commonly accepted sense of the word. They undoubtedly began as immigrants, but after they had achieved their wealth many of them moved easily between the two countries, often retaining houses and offices on both sides of the Irish Sea. Journalists occupied a similarly ambiguous position between the two societies. Many began as London reporters (particularly of parliamentary affairs) for Irish papers and later transferred to British publications. A few even established papers of their own. Among the most successful were T P O'Connor and his T P's *Weekly*, William O'Malley and his *Morning Star*, and, the most successful of all, Lord Northcliffe, who founded a string of newspapers, the most famous being the *Daily Mail*.

From the 1870s onwards fewer and later marriages reduced Irish birth-rates and consequently the numbers leaving Ireland. More women than men left the small family farms, as domestic service for the growing urban middle classes opened up new opportunities for single girls to gain respectable employment. The pattern of migration changed, too. Great Britain replaced America as the main destination after 1900. World War I and the depression dislocated the international economy and reduced the opportunity for migration. Ireland, too, was chang-

ing. Her farming underwent a transformation, with the landlord class being replaced by peasant proprietorship, and the country became an independent, but divided, state in 1921. Irish matters were no longer central in British politics and Irish journalists and politicians moved back to Dublin.

Independence sharpened the contrast between Gaelic, Roman Catholic Ireland and Anglo-Saxon, Protestant Great Britain. The two societies were moving in different directions and the Irish migrant increasingly became aware of Great Britain as a different and foreign country. One can glimpse this change in two writers' attitudes. T P O'Connor recalled that when growing up in Athlone in the 1860s he dreamed of London as a place where he might one day find work; John O'Donoghue, writing in the 1960s after a quarter of a century in Great Britain, still regarded himself as living 'In a Strange Land'.

Much had changed in the intervening century.

O'Donohue was, in fact, one of the many Irish men and women who came to Great Britain during World War II – the start of the largest wave of Irish immigrants since the last century. After the war there was a surplus of agricultural labourers, for whom there was no immediate prospect of work, a surplus caused in part by the mechanization of Irish agriculture. Great Britain on the other hand was chronically short of labour during the years of post-war reconstruction. Devastated streets had to be rebuilt, bombsites cleared, new motorways constructed, office and shopping complexes developed – the opportunities attracted hundreds of thousands of mainly young Irish, without family ties, who fitted easily into British life. The trend for more women than men to emigrate increased as the welfare state, created after 1945, offered em-

ployment for nursing and auxillary staff.

Most of these newcomers settled in the Midlands and London, reflecting shifts in the British economy away from Scotland and the north of England. In some London boroughs perhaps as many as a quarter of the citizens were Irish-born and the dance halls, pubs, and churches in those areas echoed to Irish accents. County organizations were founded for people from the same locality to meet and organize events, such as dances, annual dinners, charity events and holidays back home. Out of that social life emerged couples who married, moved out of bedsitters and put deposits on houses, had families and sent them to Roman Catholic schools and became part of the social structure of London life.

In the 1960s the Irish economy grew rapidly. But the establishment of new international companies in Ireland and grants given later to Irish farmers under the EEC's agricultural policy, though they briefly interrupted the trend of migration, did not reverse the centuries-old movement. Economic recession in the 1970s, deepening in the early 1980s brought about a resumption of emigration. None of the traditional destinations, however, provide the welcome or opportunities of previous times. In the United States and Australia quota systems reduce the numbers of those who may enter, while Great Britain's employment prospects are only marginally better than Ireland's. All this means that only the adventurous, the highly skilled and those willing to work unofficially are able to emigrate. But if opportunities abroad have declined, knowledge of what is available has increased. The international media, television and newspapers, not only make known the kind of world beyond Ireland, but more profoundly have reshaped Ireland itself. It is no longer a world of thatched cottages and turf stacks, of the 'when God made time, he made lots of it' view of life; it is now part of a wider common culture of supermarkets and factories, television and pop-music. The shock of leaving is nothing like that experienced by 19th-century or earlier emigrants. Much has undoubtedly been lost in this transformation, but it has lessened the heartache and the homesickness that echo through countless generations of song and poetry since Columba wrote in the sixth century:

I ever long for the land of Ireland
where I had power,
an exile now in the midst of strangers,
sad and tearful.

· BIBLIOGRAPHY ·

RURAL IRELAND

Estyn Evans *Irish Heritage: The Landscape, the People and their Work* (Dundalk, 1954)

Hugh Brody Inishkillane, *Change and Decline in the West of Ireland* (London, 1973)

G F Mitchell *The Irish Landscape* (London, 1976)

Timothy O'Neill *Life and Tradition in Rural Ireland* (London, 1977)

THE CHURCH

Noel Browne *Against the Tide* (Dublin, 1986)

John Cooney *The Crozier and the Dail: Church and State in Ireland 1922-1986* (Cork, 1986)

Dermot Keogh *The Vatican, the Bishops and Irish Politics 1919-1923* (Cambridge, 1986)

John Whyte *Church and State in Modern Ireland: 1923 to 1970* (Dublin, 1973)

HOUSES AND TOWNS

T B Barry *The Archaeology of Medieval Ireland* (London, 1987)

Brian de Breffny and George Mott *The Churches and Abbeys of Ireland* (London, 1976)

Maurice Craig and the Knight of Glin *Ireland Observed: A Guide to the Buildings and Antiquities of Ireland* (Cork, 1970)

Estyn Evans *Prehistoric and Early Christian Ireland: a Guide* (London, 1966)

Peter Harbison *Guide to the National Monuments of Ireland* (Dublin, 1977)

Peter Harbison, Homan Potterton and Jeanny Sheehy *Irish Art and Architecture from Prehistory to the Present* (London, 1978)

Edward Malins and the Knight of Glin *Lost Demesnes; Irish Landscape Gardening 1660-1845* (London, 1976)

Sean P O'Riordain *Antiquities of the Irish Countryside* (London, 1979)

Patrick and Maura Shaffrey *Buildings of Irish Towns* (Dublin, 1983)

IRISH INDUSTRY

James F Bradley and Brendan Dowling *Industrial Development in Northern Ireland and the Republic of Ireland* (Belfast and Dublin, 1983)

Jim Fitzpatrick and John H Kelly (eds) *Perspectives in Irish Industry* (Irish Management Institute, Dublin, 1986)

Kieran A Kennedy and John Healy *Small-Scale Manufacturing Industry in Ireland* (Dublin, 1985)

James Meenan *The Irish Economy Since 1922* (Liverpool, 1970)

IRISH LITERATURE IN THE 20TH CENTURY

Malcolm Brown *The Politics of Irish Literature* (London, 1972)

Terence Brown *Ireland: A Social and Cultural History, 1922-1979* (London, 1981)

Peter Costello *The Heart Grown Brutal: The Irish Revolution in Literature from Parnell to the Death of Yeats* (Dublin, 1977)

Seamus Deane *A Short History of Irish Literature* (London, 1986)

Douglas Dunn (ed) *Two Decades of Irish Writing* (Cheadle Hume, 1975)

Richard Fallis *The Irish Renaissance: An Introduction to Anglo-Irish Literature* (Dublin, 1978)

Robert Hogan (editor-in-chief) *The Macmillan Dictionary of Irish Literature* (London, 1979)

Benedict Kiely *Modern Irish Fiction: A Critique* (Dublin, 1950)

Frank O'Connor: *The Backward Look* (London, 1967)

IRISH MUSIC

Brendan Breathnach *Folk Music and Dances of Ireland* (Dublin, 1971)

Patrick Galvin *Irish Songs of Resistance* (London, 1962)

Bill Meek *Songs of the Irish in America* (Dublin, 1978)

John Moulden *Songs of the People* (Belfast, 1979)

Sean O'Boyle *The Irish Song Tradition* (Dublin, 1976)

Tomas O'Canainn *Traditional Music in Ireland* (London, 1978)

Colm O'Lochlainn *The Complete Irish Street Ballads* (London, 1984)

Francis O'Neill *Irish Minstrels and Musicians* (Wakefield, 1973)

Donal O'Sullivan *Carolan. The Life, Times and Music of an Irish Harper* (London, 1958)

George Zimmerman *Songs of Irish Rebellion* (Dublin, 1967)

THE TROUBLES

David Beresford *Ten Men Dead* (London, 1987)

Patrick Buckland *A History of Northern Ireland* (Dublin, 1981)

Michael Farrell *Northern Ireland: The Orange State* (London, 1976)

Ed Moloney and Andy Pollak *Paisley* (Belfast, 1986)

THE IRISH ABROAD

Ludwig Bieler *Ireland; Harbinger of the Middle Ages* (London, 1963)

David Noel Doyle *Ireland, Irishmen and Revolutionary America* (Dublin, 1981)

James E Hanley *The Irish in Modern Scotland* (Cork, 1947)

Maurice N Hennessy *The Wild Geese: The Irish Soldier in Exile* (London, 1973)

Lynn Hollen Lees *Exiles of Erin; Irish Emigrants in Victorian London* (Cornell, 1979)

Kerby A Miller *Emigrants and Exiles; Ireland and the Irish Exodus to North America* (Oxford, 1985)

John J Silke 'The Irish Abroad 1534-1691' in T W Moody, F X Martin and F J Byrne (eds) *A New History of Ireland. Vol. III* (Oxford, 1978)

J G Simms 'The Irish on the Continent 1691-1800' in T W Moody and W E Vaughan (eds) *A New History of Ireland Vol. IV* (Oxford, 1986)

Roger Swift and Sheridan Gilley (eds) *The Irish in the Victorian City* (London, 1985)

· ABOUT THE CONTRIBUTORS ·

JOHN BARRETT
SPORTING IRELAND

John Barrett was born in Tralee, County Kerry. He entered journalism with The Kerryman newspaper, Tralee in 1953.

Over the years he has been a regular contributor on GAA and greyhound affairs to national papers and magazines. He played football and hurling for Kerry as a boy and is a keen greyhound owner.

He is the son of a famous Gaelic footballer, Joe Barrett, who won six all-Ireland medals with Kerry between 1924 and 1932.

He is now a member of the editorial staff of *The Irish Post* newspaper in London.

BERNARD CANAVAN
HOUSES AND TOWNS, THE IRISH ABROAD

Bernard Canavan was born and brought up in County Longford, Ireland, and came to England in 1960. He studied Politics and Economics at Oxford University. He is a freelance designer and illustrator and is currently writing a history of London's Docklands.

JAMES DORGAN, MBA
IRISH INDUSTRY

James Dorgan is a senior economist with a leading firm of economic and management consultants. He studied economics at the National University of Ireland before taking a masters degree in business administration at Columbia University, New York. He later returned to Ireland where he joined the Confederation of Irish Industry. He has since acted as consultant to many Irish Government Departments, agencies and state companies as well as to private sector companies. He has also worked as a consultant to the World Bank, and lectured and written extensively on various aspects of the Irish economy. He is a director of Irish Steel Limited, the state-owned steel manufacturing company.

JIM O'HARA
IRISH MUSIC

Jim O'Hara was born and reared in Belfast. There was a strong tradition of music in his family, and from an early age he became interested in Irish music and song, especially that of his native Ulster. After taking a degree in history from Queen's University, Belfast, he came to London in 1966, where he now lectures in Irish history.

For a number of years, he organised Irish folk music clubs in London, and played and sang on the folk music circuit. For eight years he was a member of the well known Irish traditional music group, Tristram Shandy. He has helped to organize a series of Irish Arts festivals in London, and is deeply involved in promoting Irish studies in his present capacity as Vice-Chairman of the British Association for Irish Studies.

EAMONN HUGHES
IRISH LITERATURE IN THE 20TH CENTURY

Eamonn Hughes is currently completing research on modern Anglo-Irish autobiography at the University of Leicester. He is a member of the Executive Committee of the British Association for Irish Studies, is editor of the Association's Newsletter and joint British editor of the *Irish Literary Supplement*. He has written a number of articles on James Joyce, Patrick Kavanagh and on Irish literature in general. He is a Research Officer at the University of Nottingham.

JONATHAN MOORE
THE CHURCH, BELFAST AND ITS TROUBLES, IRISH POPULAR MUSIC

Jonathan Moore was for four years lecturer in Irish politics at York University. He is now based in London, teaching Irish studies at all educational levels. He is editor of the magazine *Irish Studies in Britain* and co-editor of the *Irish Literary Supplement.*

MARY RUSSELL
RURAL IRELAND

Mary Russell is an Irish journalist based for the most part in Oxford, Donegal and Dublin, contributing to Irish and British newspapers as well as publications in Africa and the Middle East. She has travelled extensively, most recently in the western Sahara. She spends as much time as she can in her thatched cottage in Donegal.

INDEX

176

· ACKNOWLEDGEMENTS & PICTURE CREDITS ·

The publishers would like to thank Ryanair and Murray's Rentacar, Dublin for their assistance in the production of this book.

a = above, b = below, r = right, l = left
All pictures by Trevor Wood, assisted by Jonathan Higgins, except: Irish Tourist Board pp 7l, 39r, 40, 41, 64ar, 65ar, 114, 122l, 125, 167; Illustrated London News pp 14b, 110, 137br, 152al and bl; Catholic News pp 34, 118, 164al; National Library of Ireland pp 53, 94br; Ian Howes pp 58l and b, 59, 84ar and br, 85a, 165ar and br; Victoria and Albert Museum p 66; Ireland Industrial Development Authority pp 70, 73, 79a, 83b, 88al and ar, 96 bl and br, 97r; Library of Congress, Washington D C pp 74, 117br, 145br, 16l, 164br, 166; Guinness pp 80ar and al, 81 middle, 89a; Robert Opie Collection pp 80b, 84bl, 85r; Geray Sweeney, Impact Photos pp 96a, 108, 112, 116, 121, 123b, 127, 155; Mark Gerson p 113; National Archives, Washington D C p 122r; Phonogram Press p 129; All Sport pp 130, 133, 134, 136br, 139, 144; Steve Bacon p 135r; Keystone Press Agency p 136b; Mrs Vincent O'Brien p 136 top; Ed Byrne p 137al; The Mansell Collection p 137ar; British Library p 145bl; Cognizance Heraldic Artwork Agency p 154; New York Historical Society p 160; New York City Convention and Visitors' Board, New York City p 162; Museum of the City of New York p 163bl; *Puck* magazine, 24 May, 1882 p 163ar.